Welcome to the World of Scene-A-Rama™

The Scene-A-Rama™ Project Book provides you with the motivation, stimulation and inspiration for building amazing dioramas and displays. Instead of just step-by-step instruction for a few select projects that will end up looking like all the others in your class, the ideas in this book (and your imagination) will help you make your own unique creations.

- **Great for any subject** – Math, Science, English, History and more!
- **Great for any student** – Preschool to high school, college and beyond!
- **Great for any project** – Volcanoes, masks, Indian villages, storybooks, mobiles, missions and much more!

Introduction

Project Ideas

Throughout this book, project ideas (along with helpful tips and techniques) are marked with this Light Bulb icon.

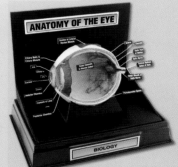

Building Basics

Scene-A-Rama™ Product Line

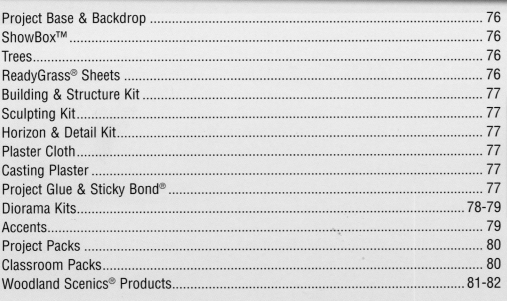

Welcome

To use this book, read through and pick up ideas for your diorama or display. These projects are only a very small sampling of what you can do when you use your imagination. Look for the light bulb icon, which gives you easy tips, techniques and suggestions. On most pages we give you a suggested materials list. You will find that Scene-A-Rama offers complete kits with everything you need. We've made it simple.

Let your imagination go as you do your research, plan your project, gather your supplies and build your diorama! The examples and ideas in this book can be applied to any project in some way, but don't be afraid to make your diorama or display even more unique and special - unlike anything your teacher has ever seen!

You can get everything you need for your dioramas from the Scene-A-Rama line. Use the complete line of products to make your diorama the best it can be. If you would like additional products, you can purchase them at **www.woodlandscenics.com.**

➡ Project Guidelines

Do Your Research

If you have an assignment guide from your teacher, be sure to read it carefully and include everything on the list. Research as much information as you can about your subject. Go to the library and look in non-fiction books and encyclopedias. You can also check on the Internet, ask your family members or experts. Keep a list of your resources on a separate sheet of paper.

Think about all of the important parts of your research. For example, if you are doing research on American Indians consider each of the following items and keep a list of the important ones.

- Shelter/Home
- Food/Water
- Landscape/Terrain

- Clothing
- Predators
- Climate

- Environment
- Time Period
- Location

- Major Events
- Effects on History
- Employment

Utilize the Web Site

During every stage of planning and building your project our helpful Web site, www.scenearama.com, will motivate you with ideas, technical tips and suggestions, how-to videos, photos, illustrations and tons of inspiration to help you to get your assignment completed.

Visit www.scenearama.com

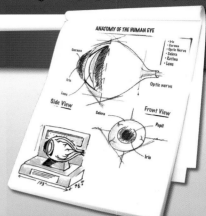

Plan Your Project

Look through the pages of this book for ideas on making any project and then draw your ideas out on a sheet of paper. Be sure to label important parts and where certain items will be on your project. Use your research to add unique or interesting items. For example, if you are making a diagram of the eye, label the important parts like the cornea, pupil and iris. Look up eye trivia on the Internet and find a unique fact that you could put on your project. Go to the www.scenearama.com **Project Gallery**. There you will find hundreds of photos that will spark your imagination or solve your project planning dilemma.

Gather Your Supplies

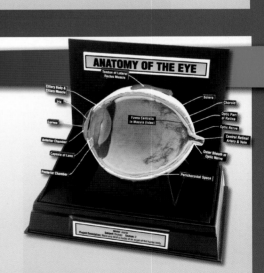

When you decide on the project you will be making, go to scenearama.com and click **Products** to see our complete line of products, kit contents, instructions and other important information. Then visit your hobby shop to select Scene-A-Rama products. Scene-A-Rama kits have basically everything you need, but the following tools and materials will make assembly easier:

- Scissors
- Straightedge
- Hobby knife
- Tape
- Paper towels
- Water
- Pencil
- Common household materials
- Other products available from Woodland Scenics (see page 82 for details).

Build Your Project

Before you start your project, make sure you have completed this checklist:
- Read your assignment guide carefully
- Finish your research
- Draw out your plan
- Gather your supplies and materials

Go to www.scenearama.com to watch the how-to demonstrations. You'll learn how to easily build mountains, volcanoes, make buildings, sculpt about anything and so much more!

You will also find downloadable **Backgrounds & Patterns** to make great backdrops for your project. Now, let's get started building your project, but most of all...have fun!

Project Base & Backdrop

The Project Base & Backdrop makes a great foundation for dioramas, displays or school projects. This product allows you to create a spectacular display base with a backdrop. You can also modify it to make a shadowbox for collections and more!

The plastic Base includes a placard to label your project. The Backdrop is a white, one-piece folded backer that allows you to paint, decorate, label or use as is. Four pieces of double-stick tape are included for Backdrop assembly. The Project Base & Backdrop is available in two sizes and includes labels, double-sided tape and easy instructions.

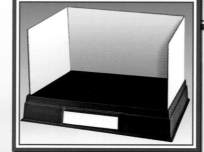

Patent Pending

Large Project Base & Backdrop (above)
The project area of the plastic base is 16 $\frac{1}{4}$"w x 10 $\frac{3}{4}$"d x 11"h and the overall size is 18"w x 12 $\frac{1}{2}$"d x 13 $\frac{1}{8}$"h.

Small Project Base & Backdrop (left)
The project area of the plastic base is 10 $\frac{3}{4}$"w x 7 $\frac{3}{8}$"d x 7 $\frac{1}{2}$"h and the overall size is 12 $\frac{1}{2}$"w x 9 $\frac{1}{4}$"d x 9 $\frac{5}{8}$"h.

Use for Dioramas & Displays!

Use as a Shadowbox!

ShowBox™

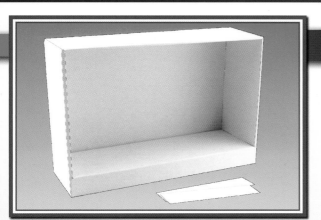

The ShowBox is great for shoebox dioramas! It is made of durable, white material and stands up to the bus ride to and from school. Just build the diorama inside and paint, decorate or label the outside.

Labels and easy instructions are included.

ShowBox (above) The overall size of the ShowBox is 13 ½"w x 4 ½"d x 10"h (inside dimensions - 13"w x 4 ½"d x 8 ½"h).

Use as a Shoebox Diorama!

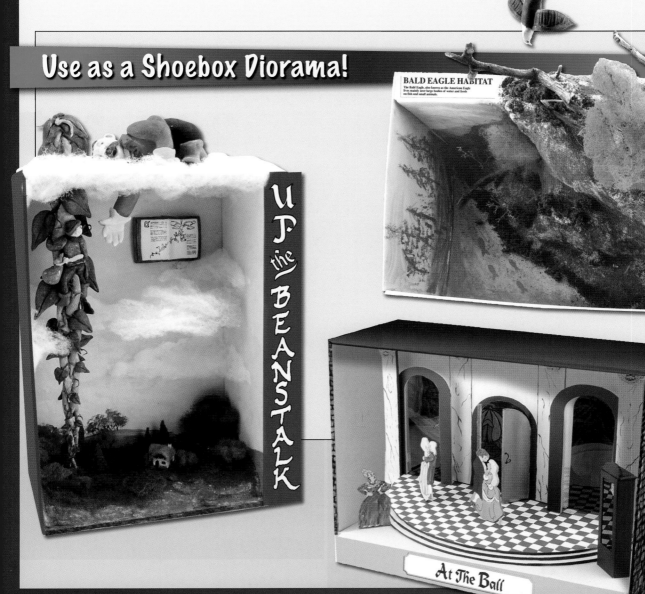

Outer Space

The Solar System is an easy and fun school project to make. Pick out one particular planet like Jupiter and do a project about it. There are lots of facts and myths about planets, so do your research to try to find interesting and unique information about them. Here are some examples of projects using planets: Planetary Alignment, Distance Between Planets, The Milky Way, Black Holes in Space or Moon Phases.

Planetary Alignment Shoebox Diorama

Everything you need to make a planetary alignment diorama is included in the Sculpting Kit. Sculpt planets with the Sculpting Clay. Use Project Paints to color the planets and Project Wire to suspend them. Display your Solar System inside a ShowBox.

An easy way to remember the planets and their placement in the Solar System is to use a fun phrase:

Many **V**ery **E**nergetic **M**onkeys **J**ust **S**wing **U**ntil **N**ightfall!

Mercury, **V**enus, **E**arth, **M**ars, **J**upiter, **S**aturn, **U**ranus and **N**eptune!

SOLAR SYSTEM

Suggested Materials:
• ShowBox
• Sculpting Kit

Sphere of the Earth's Core

Cover a wad of newspaper with Plaster Cloth to make the Earth or other planets. Depending on the size of your project, you may need to strengthen it by applying additional Plaster Cloth. Don't forget to add raised areas where there are mountain ranges. Cut out a section of the Earth's sphere to show the inner core, the outer core and the Earth's crust, which can be sculpted with clay. Use several shades of the same color to show these inner layers. Be sure to do your research so you can properly identify them. Paint the land and water features and label your project.

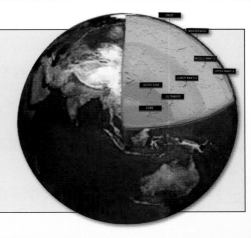

Planet Making Tip

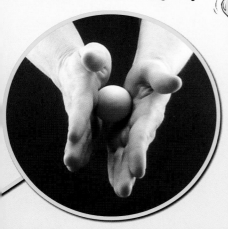

To make the roundest planet possible, roll the clay lightly between your palms.

Hanging Solar System Mobile

Create a hanging Solar System mobile, using clay from the Sculpting Kit. Use a very fine fishing line or thread to hang the planets from a sturdy wire.

Suggested Materials:
- Sculpting Kit
- Thick wire and fishing line or thread

Suspension Technique

Use Project Wire, included in the Sculpting Kit, to suspend planets and add labels to your diorama or display.

Did You Know?

Have you ever noticed the dark spots on the moon? These spots were caused by comets and asteroids that crashed into the Moon. They broke the surface rock causing lava to ooze out, and the dark spots you see are just ancient beds of cooled lava.

Anatomy

The anatomy of the human body holds many systems: skeletal, digestive, muscular, lymphatic, reproductive, nervous, cardiovascular and endocrine. Within those systems are thousands of subjects you can use for school projects, such as the eye. The Project Base & Backdrop is perfect for making dioramas or displays of the anatomy. Use Plaster Cloth and the Sculpting Kit to create your subject.

Anatomy of the Human Heart

You can form a heart diagram easily with Plaster Cloth and the materials from the Sculpting Kit. Depending on the size of your project, you may need to strengthen it by applying additional Plaster Cloth. Wad newspapers into the shape of a heart and cover with Plaster Cloth. When dry, cut the heart shape in half and take out the newspaper. Sculpt the four chambers of the heart and the arteries with Sculpting Clay and the Sculpting Tool. Paint the heart with Project Paints.

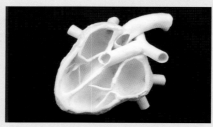
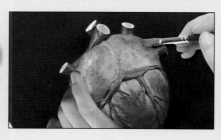
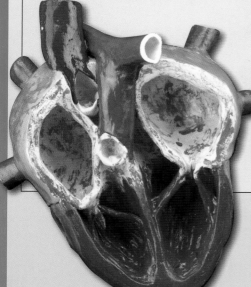

Suggested Materials:
- Newspaper
- Plaster Cloth
- Sculpting Kit (Project Paints included!)

Lens Tip

Special materials, like the Clear Plastic used for the lens, are included in the Building & Structure Kit.

Muscles & Nerves

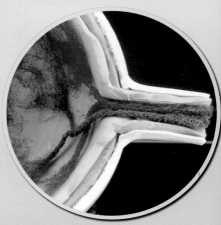

Sculpt the inside layers of the eye with Sculpting Clay. Paint the tiny nerves with Project Paints.

Did You Know?

- Every day the heart pumps about 1,500-2,000 gallons of blood through the adult human body. That amount of blood would fill an oval pool approximately 10' long x 8' wide x 4' deep!
- Babies cry, but they don't produce tears until they are one to three months old!

How Did They Do That?

Plaster Cloth

Sculpting Clay

Cover a medium balloon with Plaster Cloth (three or more layers is recommended).

Allow to dry, cut in half and sand until smooth.

Use Sculpting Clay to form inner layers, then paint.

Glue layers into place. Mount and label your project.

💡 Parts of the Eye

Make a model of the human eye and display it on a base with labels for all of the parts.

Suggested Materials:
• Project Base & Backdrop
• Medium balloon
• Plaster Cloth
• Sculpting Kit

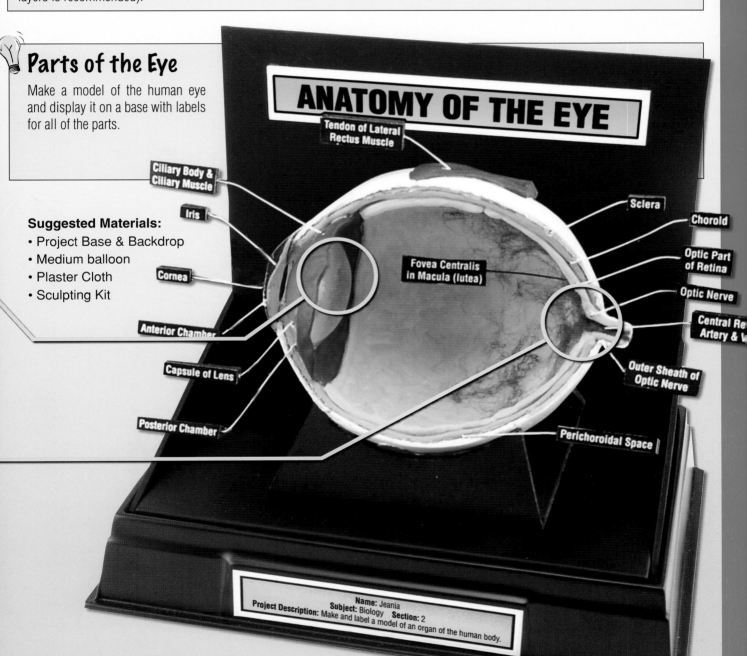

ANATOMY OF THE EYE

Tendon of Lateral Rectus Muscle

Ciliary Body & Ciliary Muscle

Iris

Cornea

Anterior Chamber

Capsule of Lens

Posterior Chamber

Fovea Centralis in Macula (lutea)

Sclera

Choroid

Optic Part of Retina

Optic Nerve

Central Re Artery & V

Outer Sheath of Optic Nerve

Perichoroidal Space

Name: Jeania
Subject: Biology   **Section:** 2
Project Description: Make and label a model of an organ of the human body.

Molecular Anatomy

It's fun and easy to make cell and DNA structures with the Sculpting Kit, Plaster Cloth and other Scene-A-Rama products. Remember, there are different types of cells, such as human, animal, plant and others that don't have the same structure. DNA chains are also as individual as people and their fingerprints. Make your project as unique and individual as you can!

Structure of a Cell Diagram

Create the cell by wadding newspapers in a cell shape. Cover the newspaper with Plaster Cloth, creating the outside of the cell. Depending on the size of your project, you may need to strengthen it by applying additional Plaster Cloth. Sculpt cell pieces with materials from the Sculpting Kit, which includes Sculpting Clay, a Sculpting Tool, Project Paints and more.

Cell Parts

Paint the cell pieces bright colors with the Project Paints.

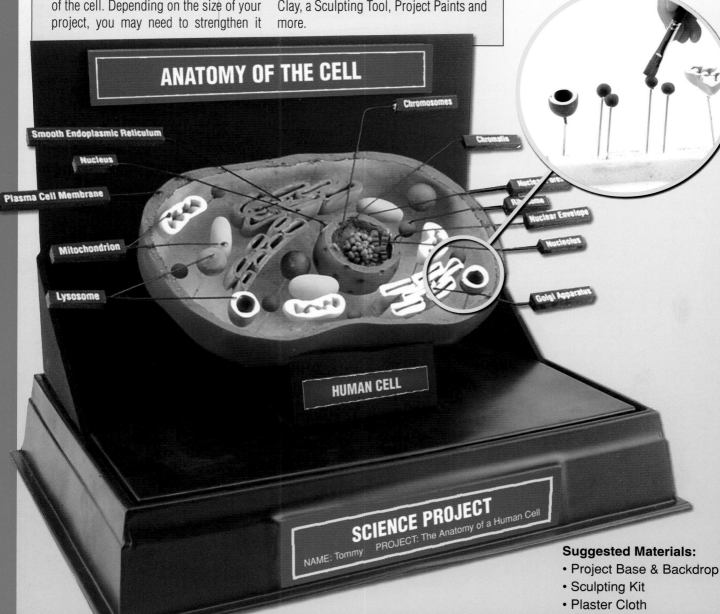

ANATOMY OF THE CELL

Chromosomes

Smooth Endoplasmic Reticulum

Chromatin

Nucleus

Nuclear Pore

Plasma Cell Membrane

Ribosome

Nuclear Envelope

Mitochondrion

Nucleolus

Lysosome

Golgi Apparatus

HUMAN CELL

SCIENCE PROJECT
NAME: Tommy   PROJECT: The Anatomy of a Human Cell

Suggested Materials:
- Project Base & Backdrop
- Sculpting Kit
- Plaster Cloth

14

Tectonic Plates

The Earth's top layer, the lithosphere, is broken up into "tectonic plates." There are seven major plates on the earth's outer layer, plus many smaller ones. Many natural events (including earthquakes and volcanoes) happen often at the plate boundaries because of the shifting plates. Scientists say that these tectonic plates move very, very slowly: approximately 8.5 centimeters a year. That is just a little more than 3 ½ inches!

💡 Tectonic Plates

Suggested Materials:
- Project Base & Backdrop
- Water Diorama Kit
- Building & Structure Kit

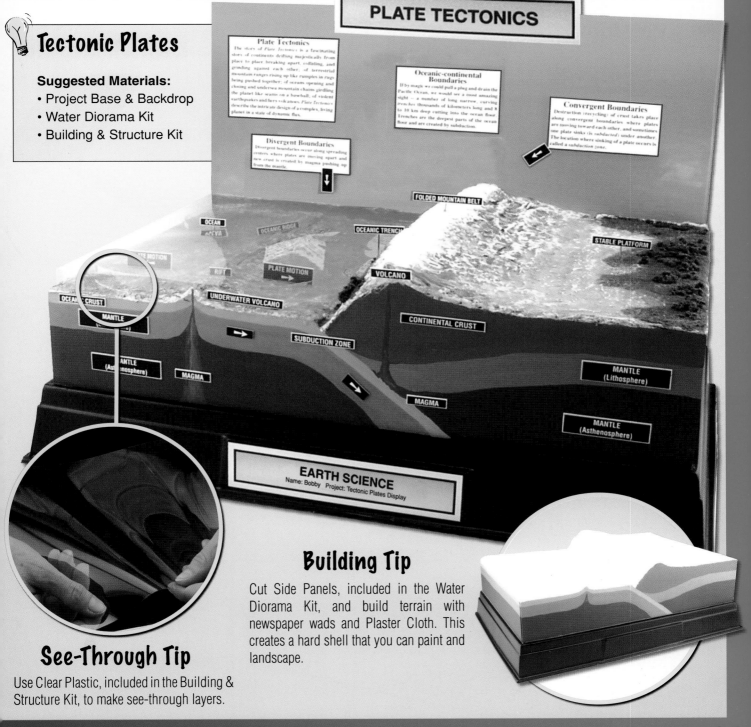

See-Through Tip

Use Clear Plastic, included in the Building & Structure Kit, to make see-through layers.

Building Tip

Cut Side Panels, included in the Water Diorama Kit, and build terrain with newspaper wads and Plaster Cloth. This creates a hard shell that you can paint and landscape.

15

Volcanoes

There are several types of volcanoes: Composite Volcanoes - also called stratovolcanoes, are formed by alternating layers of lava and rock fragments; Shield Volcanoes – are broad, gently sloping cones built by layers of lava flows; and Cinder Cone Volcanoes are steep, cone-shaped hills formed over a volcano vent. Volcanoes can be active or dormant. Volcanoes that have recent activity are called active volcanoes. These volcanoes have either erupted or have had lava flows in the last 100 or so years. Volcanoes that have not had recent activity are called dormant or sleeping volcanoes. These volcanoes are usually grown over with vegetation.

Erupting Volcano

Use the Mountain Diorama Kit to make an erupting volcano. Form your volcano (using newspaper wads and Plaster Cloth) around the volcano tube that's included in the kit. Add 1 teaspoon of baking soda to the tube. In a separate container (use an eyedropper), add 3-4 drops of liquid dish detergent to 1 ounce of vinegar. The dish detergent makes the flow last longer.

Add 6 drops each of red and yellow food coloring to the vinegar mixture to make the lava orange. Pour 1/2 of the vinegar mixture in the volcano tube to create an eruption. When the flow slows down, add the remaining mixture. When finished, empty contents and reuse.

Note: Perform this experiment only with adult supervision.

Suggested Materials:
• Mountain Diorama Kit
• Water, food coloring, liquid dish detergent, baking soda and vinegar

Rock Making Tip

The Mountain Diorama Kit includes a Rock Mold, Casting Plaster and Rock Colors for making and coloring your own rocks.

Lava Flow Technique

Use Casting Plaster, included in the Mountain Diorama Kit, to make a lava flow. Lava cools from the top, so paint the top gray and the bottom red and orange.

Did You Know?

Molten rock that is still underground and hasn't erupted is called "magma." Once it has erupted above the surface, it is called "lava."

How Did They Do That?

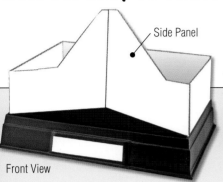

Side Panel

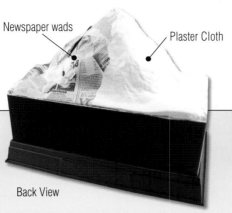

Newspaper wads

Plaster Cloth

Casting Plaster

Rocks

Front View

Start with the Project Base & Backdrop and the Mountain Diorama Kit. Cut the Side Panels and glue into place.

Back View

Build up the volcano with newspaper wads and cover with Plaster Cloth.

Finished

Add rocks, rock color, foliage and labels. Pour Casting Plaster down the sides and paint to look like lava.

360° View (Cut away) Volcano

This diorama is built to be viewed from all sides. If you can put the diorama on a spinning base, your viewers can turn the volcano to see the activity inside.

Suggested Materials:
• Project Base & Backdrop
• Mountain Diorama Kit
• Horizon & Detail Kit

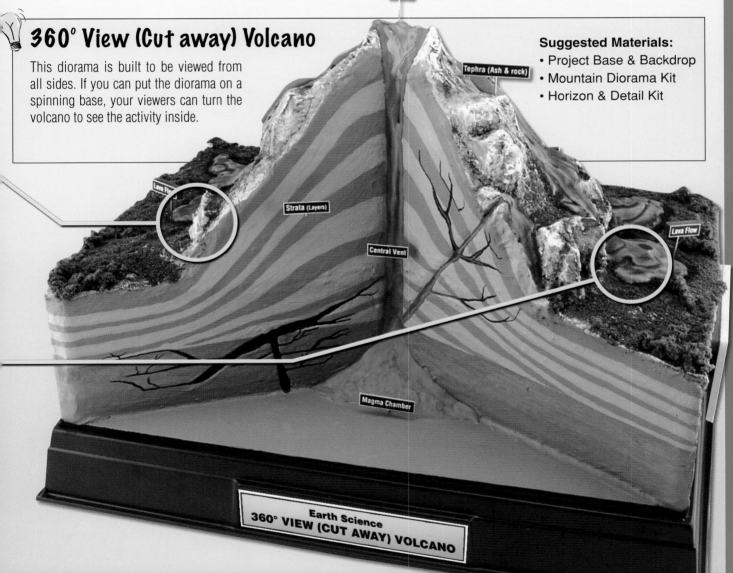

Crater

Tephra (Ash & rock)

Lava Flow

Strata (Layers)

Central Vent

Lava Flow

Magma Chamber

Earth Science
360° VIEW (CUT AWAY) VOLCANO

Weather

Build a diorama showing different weather patterns, effects of erosion, types of natural disasters and so on. You can even display an experiment, like a barometer or rain gauge, on the Project Base. Display your recordings on the Backdrop.

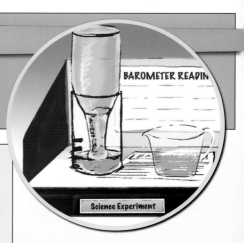

BAROMETER READIN

Science Experiment

Effects of Erosion Diorama

Show the effects of erosion on a hillside and compare them to a weather treated environment using the Water Diorama Kit. Paint the water area with Water Undercoat.

To make muddy water, mix in brown paint. Pour Realistic Water on top. Make sure to label your project. Add realistic details like trees and Dead Fall to your diorama.

Effects of lateral water erosion on stream banks
1. The swiftly-moving water from a sudden storm erodes the bank.
2. Trees fall into the waterway, damming it up.
3. The water finds a new way around the trees and washes away sedimentary layers of rock.
4. The sediment is carried away and causes buildup downstream, potentially harming the stream's ecosystem.
5. Creates a dangerous landslide area for people enjoying water-related activities like fishing and canoeing.

Effects of adding rocks (riprap) and vegetation to stream banks
1. The rocks hold the soils in place.
2. The vegetation takes root to help hold the soils in place.
3. No trees are damming up the waterway.
4. Allows safer wildlife habitats.
5. People can enjoy water-related activities and the beauty of the area.

Overhanging River Bank

Tree Roots

Cracks In The Soil

Collapsed River Bank

Tree From River Bank

Brown Water

Riprap

Clear Water

EFFECTS OF EROSION
By: Eric Subject: Earth Science

Suggested Materials:
• Project Base & Backdrop
• Water Diorama Kit
• Conifer & Deciduous Trees

Puffy Clouds

Make clouds for any weather diorama or display with Puffy Clouds, included in the Horizon & Detail Kit.

Special Effects

Use the Building & Structure Kit to add signs and labels to your diorama.

Clear Plastic

Create effects, like this layer of rain, by etching or painting Clear Plastic, included in the Building & Structure Kit.

Weather

Suggested Materials:

- Project Base & Backdrop
- Water Diorama Kit
- Horizon & Detail Kit
- Building & Structure Kit

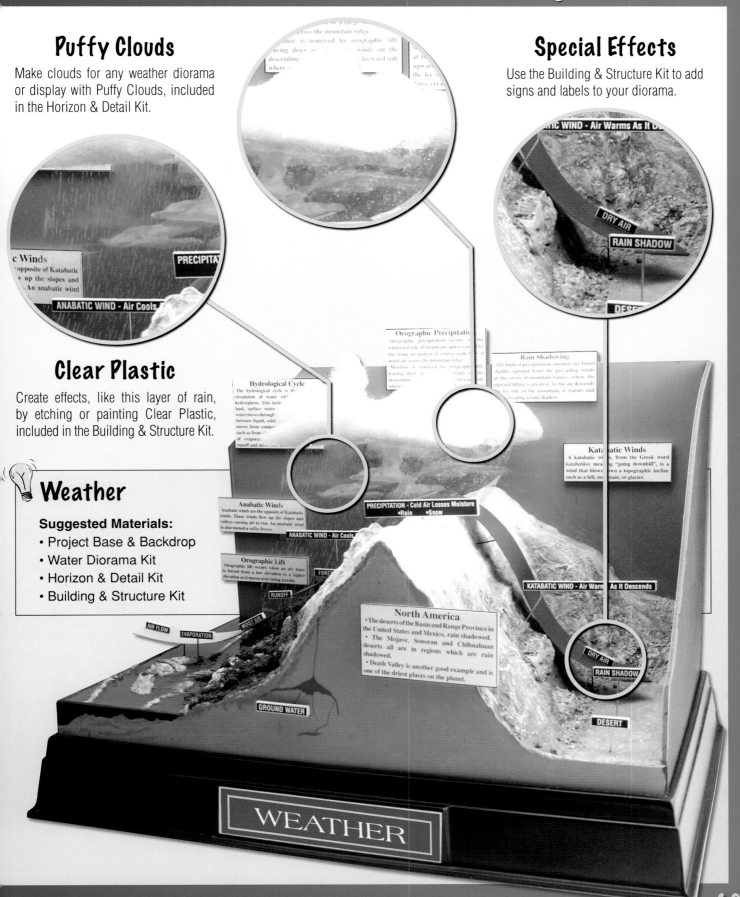

Orographic Precipitation
Orographic precipitation occurs on the windward side of mountains and is caused by the rising air motion of a large scale flow of moist air across the mountain ridge. Moisture is removed by orographic lift, leaving drier air on the down winds on the descending, leeward side where...

Rain Shadowing
The highest precipitation amounts are found slightly upwind from the prevailing winds at the crests of mountain ranges, where the upward lifting is greatest. As the air descends the lee side of the mountain, it warms and dries creating a rain shadow.

Hydrological Cycle
The hydrological cycle is the circulation of water within the hydrosphere. This includes land, surface water, water moves through between liquid, solid moves from components such as from of evapora... runoff and subsur...

Katabatic Winds
A katabatic wind, from the Greek word *katabatikos* meaning "going downhill", is a wind that blows down a topographic incline such as a hill, mountain, or glacier.

Anabatic Winds
Anabatic winds are the opposite of Katabatic winds. These winds flow up the slopes and valleys causing air to rise. An anabatic wind is also named a valley breeze.

Orographic Lift
Orographic lift occurs when an air mass is forced from a low elevation to a higher elevation as it moves over rising terrain.

PRECIPITATION - Cold Air Losses Moisture
•Rain   •Snow

ANABATIC WIND - Air Cools

KATABATIC WIND - Air Warms As It Descends

RUNOFF

FOREST

North America
• The deserts of the Basin and Range Province in the United States and Mexico, rain shadowed.
• The Mojave, Sonoran and Chihuahuan deserts all are in regions which are rain shadowed.
• Death Valley is another good example and is one of the driest places on the planet.

DRY AIR

RAIN SHADOW

DESERT

AIR FLOW   EVAPORATION   MOIST AIR

GROUND WATER

WEATHER

ANABATIC WIND - Air Cools

PRECIPITA

DRY AIR

RAIN SHADOW

Caves

Caves are holes in our earth's surface, which are usually large enough for a person to enter. Most caves are formed by the action of water on soft rock. Volcanoes and earthquakes also help caves form. Where there is limestone, there is usually a cave, or a cave in the process. Caves usually hold clues to how prehistoric humans and animals lived. Russell Cave in Alabama shows evidence of humans that lived 9,000 years ago.

Stalactites and Stalagmites

Stalagmites are mounded deposits of calcium (from dripping water) that slowly build up on the floor of a cave. Stalactites hang from the ceiling or sides of a cave. An easy way to remember: "stalactites stick *tight* to the top!"

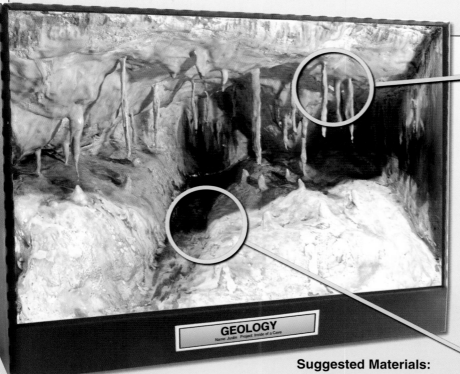

GEOLOGY
Name: Justin   Project: Inside of a Cave

Suggested Materials:
- ShowBox
- Plaster Cloth
- Casting Plaster
- Ripplin' Water Kit

Stalactites & Stalagmites

To create stalactites, roll wet Plaster Cloth and attach it to the cave ceiling. Allow it to dry and apply Casting Plaster around the Plaster Cloth. Let the Plaster drip to make stalagmites.

Water Technique

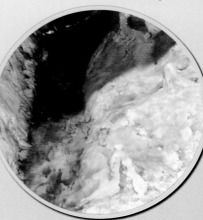

Add Realistic Water, available in the Ripplin' Water Kit, to the cave floor, walls and other surfaces to give it a damp, cave atmosphere.

Did You Know?

Mammoth Cave in Kentucky is the world's longest system of caves. It extends approximately 350 miles!

How Did They Do That?

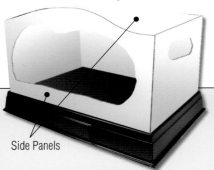

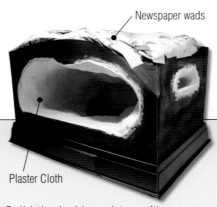

Newspaper wads

Side Panels

Plaster Cloth

Casting Plaster

Assemble the Project Base & Backdrop. Add Side Panels, included in the Mountain Diorama Kit, to the top and front.

Build the inside and top with newspaper wads. Tape the newspaper in place and cover with Plaster Cloth.

Add rocks, foliage, trees and more. Use Casting Plaster to make stalactites and stalagmites.

💡 **Cave**

CAVE-DWELLERS' HABITAT
Geology Project Name: Mark Grade: 7 Mr. Farris

Suggested Materials:
- Project Base & Backdrop
- Mountain Diorama Kit
- Deciduous Trees

Dinosaurs

Building a Dinosaur Diorama can be fun and educational. There are lots of research areas that you can choose for your project, including: Types of Dinosaurs, a Geological Timeline and Dinosaur Habitats or Fossils. The study of fossils is called Paleontology. Animal fossils are divided into two categories: body parts (bones, claws, teeth, skin, embryos, etc.) and traces (footprints, nests, dung, tooth marks, etc.).

Dinosaur Habitat

The Horizon & Detail Kit includes Project Paints, Puffy Clouds and Foliage Fiber for detailing your habitat with clouds, smoke, foliage and a horizon.

Suggested Materials:
- Project Base & Backdrop
- Horizon & Detail Kit
- Green Grass ReadyGrass
- Palm Trees

Flying Creatures

Make flying creatures with the clay in the Sculpting Kit. Use the Project Wire in the kit to suspend your animals.

PREHISTORIC TIMES

Water Effects

Make long or short waterfalls, waves and ripples using the materials in the Water Diorama Kit.

Did You Know?

The dinosaur with the longest name - micropachycephalosaurus - is also one of the smallest dinosaurs!

💡 Fossils

Create great plant and animal fossils using the Sculpting Kit. Take a leaf or shell and press it into the Sculpting Clay. Let it dry and use Project Paint to make it look like a real fossil.

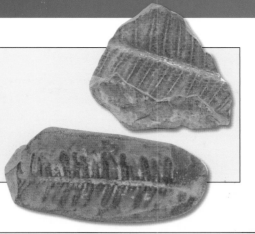

"In the Water" Technique

Sculpt and paint your dinosaur without legs. Pour a thin layer of Realistic Water around the dinosaur and allow it to dry.

💡 The Jurassic Period

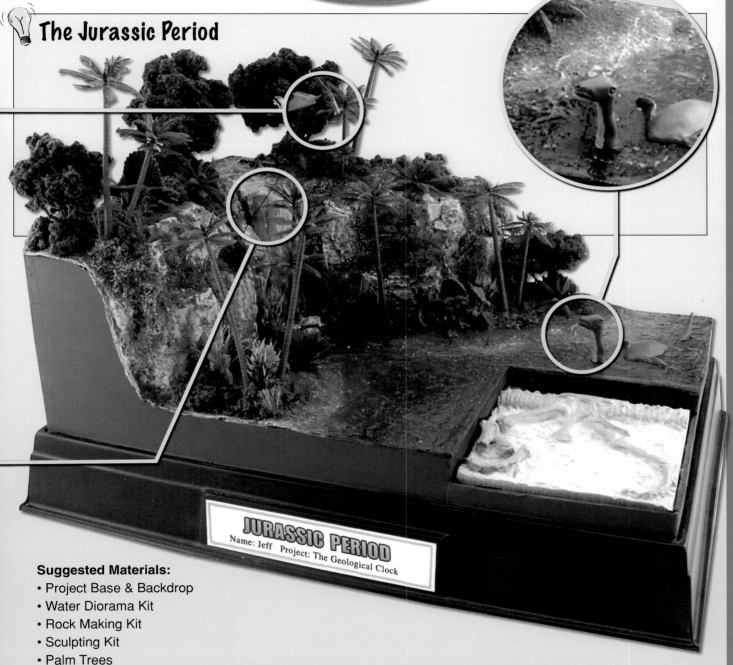

JURASSIC PERIOD
Name: Jeff   Project: The Geological Clock

Suggested Materials:
- Project Base & Backdrop
- Water Diorama Kit
- Rock Making Kit
- Sculpting Kit
- Palm Trees

Endangered Species

In 1973, Congress passed the Endangered Species Act to help protect wildlife from becoming extinct. According to the US Fish and Wildlife Service, the Act is meant to protect threatened species all over the world, while also conserving the environments they live in. Use the Project Base & Backdrop to create your own endangered species habitats and fill them with sculptures of endangered animals.

Sculpt Animals

It's easy to sculpt animals with the Sculpting Kit. Begin with a basic shape, then pinch and pull the clay to form the facial features. Form the arms and legs and push them onto the body. Then begin shaping the face, fingers and toes and creating detail with the Sculpting Tool. When you're done, add special details from the Sculpting Kit like Project Paint and Fun Fur!

Suggested Materials:
• Sculpting Kit

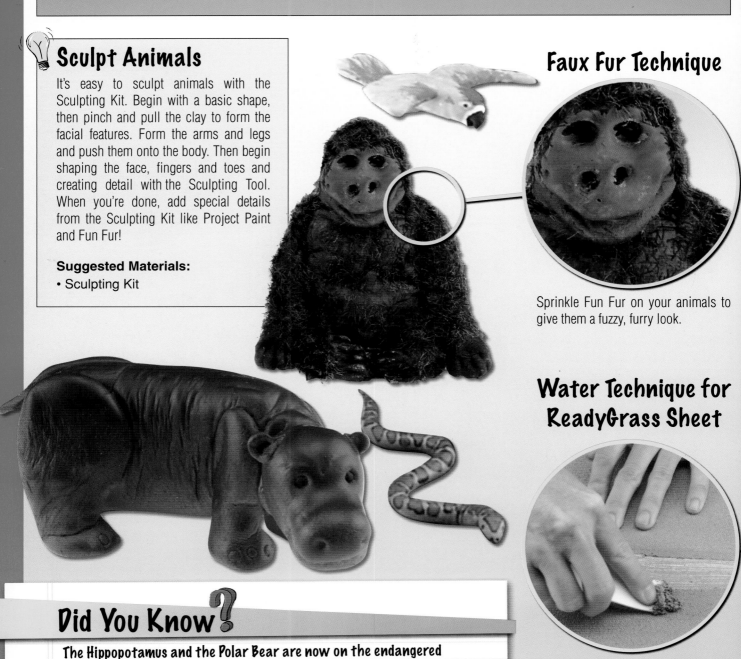

Faux Fur Technique

Sprinkle Fun Fur on your animals to give them a fuzzy, furry look.

Water Technique for ReadyGrass Sheet

To make water areas on ReadyGrass Sheets, wet the area and scrape off the turf, creating a flat area to add water.

Did You Know?

The Hippopotamus and the Polar Bear are now on the endangered species list and are threatened by extinction.

Suspension Tip

Backdrop Tip

Paint your backdrop to create an environment. The Horizon & Detail Kit has a variety of paint colors to choose from.

Suspend a bird, fish, sign or other item with the Project Wire, included in the Sculpting Kit.

💡 Endangered Species

Suggested Materials:
• Project Base & Backdrop
• Desert Oasis Diorama Kit
• Sculpting Kit
• Horizon & Detail Kit

ENDANGERED SPECIES OF SOUTH AFRICA
• Rosie Parrot   • Mountain Gorilla
• Hippopotamus   • Blue Cranes
• African Elephant   • Rock Python

Subject: Biology   Name: Daniel   Grade 9

Animal Habitats

Animals need to live in environments (habitats) that support their needs (just like humans do) with water, food and shelter. Some animals depend on certain species of other plants and animals. For instance, scientists say that one Spotted Owl needs at least 3,000 acres of "old-growth" forest to survive. This environment offers cool, damp conditions, with plenty of holes and cavities to roost in. These trees are home to lots of rodents, which are one of the owl's main food sources.

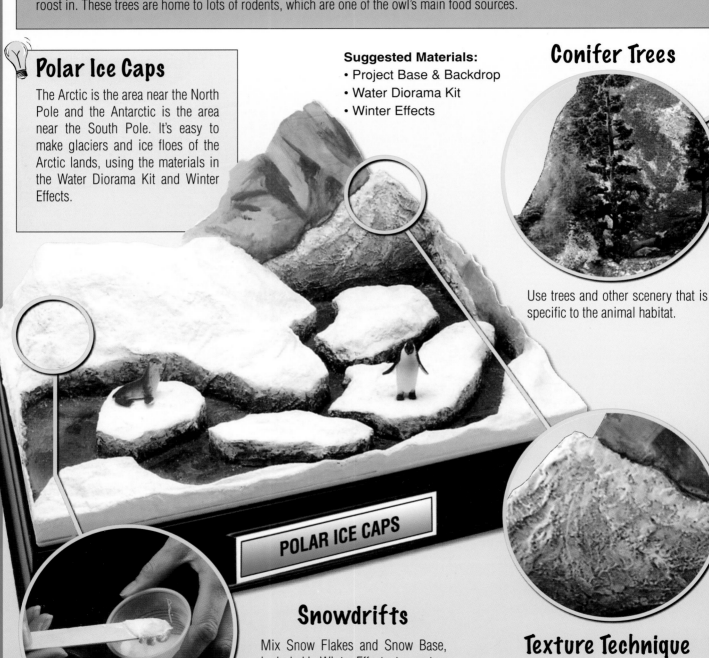

Polar Ice Caps

The Arctic is the area near the North Pole and the Antarctic is the area near the South Pole. It's easy to make glaciers and ice floes of the Arctic lands, using the materials in the Water Diorama Kit and Winter Effects.

Suggested Materials:
- Project Base & Backdrop
- Water Diorama Kit
- Winter Effects

POLAR ICE CAPS

Conifer Trees

Use trees and other scenery that is specific to the animal habitat.

Snowdrifts

Mix Snow Flakes and Snow Base, included in Winter Effects, to create a mixture perfect for snowdrifts.

Texture Technique

Use Plaster Cloth on the backdrop to make rock textures or icebergs.

Mountain Environment

Make a realistic diorama to display an animal habitat using the Water Diorama Kit. Add black bears fishing in a stream, or deer hiding in the woods.

Suggested Materials:
- Project Base & Backdrop
- Water Diorama Kit
- Conifer Trees

MOUNTAIN ENVIRONMENT
NAME: Andy   SUBJECT: Geography

Labels

The Project Base & Backdrop and the ShowBox include labels with adhesive on the back. Make your label simple, or get creative.

Bald Eagle Habitat

Suggested Materials:
- ShowBox
- Horizon & Detail Kit

BALD EAGLE HABITAT

The Bald Eagle, also known as the American Eagle lives mainly near large bodies of water and feeds on fish and small animals.

Ocean Life

The sea is full of colorful fish, shellfish, squid, corals, starfish, octopus and much more. Just one species of fish can have many variations in its family. Creatures in the sea are easy to sculpt because they are usually long and narrow with short fins and tails. They are also fun to paint, because they are full of bright, vivid colors. Use your imagination to create a cool underwater scene!

Marine Life

"Out of Water" Tip

Sculpt a dolphin and cut it in half. Glue each half to opposite sides of a clear surface. It will look like the dolphin is half in the water and half out.

Making Waves

Apply Water Effects to any surface (like clear Plexiglas®) and use a Stir Stick to make waves by patting gently, up and down. It dries clear!

Suggested Materials:
• Project Base & Backdrop
• Water Diorama Kit
• Sculpting Kit

OCEAN LIFE   Marty

Sculpting Plant Life

Sculpt plant life with Sculpting Clay. Push clay through a screen to make coral tubes.

Sculpting Marine Life

Make dolphins, stingrays, sharks and more with the Sculpting Kit. Use the Sculpting Tool to add details like eyes and gills. The kit also includes Project Paint to finish your creatures.

Shoebox Aquarium

Suggested Materials:
• ShowBox
• Sculpting Kit
• Desert Sand ReadyGrass Sheet

ReadyGrass Rocks

Wrap Desert Sand ReadyGrass Sheets around newspaper wads to create large rocks.

29

Water Scenes

Moving or falling water is one of the strongest forces in the universe. Hydropower is the process of using the energy of falling water (from dams, waterwheels or other turbines) to make electricity. Long ago, waterwheels were used to power sawmills and gristmills. Some waterwheels are still in use today. You can build a waterwheel with the Building & Structure Kit. Label the working parts, showing where and how the power is made.

💡 Waterfall Diorama

You can create a beautiful waterfall scene using the Water Diorama Kit. It's easy to make any kind of moving water effect: waterfalls, rapids, water falling from waterwheels and much more. Add animals or people to complete your diorama.

WATERFALL DIORAMA

Suggested Materials:
• Project Base & Backdrop
• Water Diorama Kit

Waterfalls & Rapids

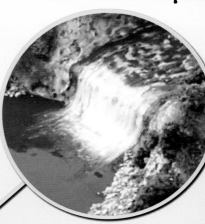

Use Water Effects and Realistic Water, included in the Water Diorama Kit, to make realistic still or moving water effects.

Structures

The Project Sticks and Project Glue, included in the Building & Structure Kit, are great for building any structure.

Did You Know❓

People have been using waterpower in gristmills for more than 2,000 years. Gristmills grind grain, such as corn, wheat and oats.

How Did They Do That?

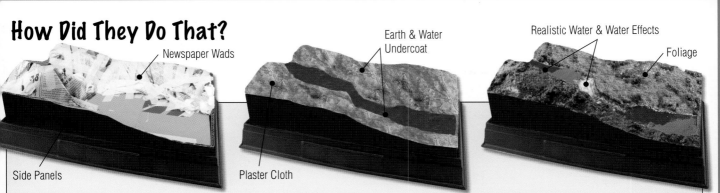

Newspaper Wads

Side Panels

Earth & Water Undercoat

Plaster Cloth

Realistic Water & Water Effects

Foliage

Cut Side Panels, included in the Water Diorama Kit, and glue onto base. Use newspaper wads to build terrain.

Cover with Plaster Cloth, allow to dry and paint on Earth and Water Undercoats.

Pour Realistic Water and add Water Effects, then add foliage, rocks, bushes and more.

Autumn Trees

Add Autumn Trees to any diorama to establish a seasonal setting.

💡 Water Mill

Make a diorama that demonstrates water power. Model it after a historic mill or create your own!

HISTORIC BRIDGETOWN WATER MILL

Suggested Materials:
• Project Base & Backdrop
• Water Diorama Kit
• Building & Structure Kit
• Autumn Trees

Indian Civilizations

There are thousands of Indian tribes and civilizations, to name just a few: North American Indians (Cherokee, Inuit, Osage, Eskimos, Pueblos, etc.) and South American Indians (Mayas, Toltecs and Aztecs), plus hundreds of tribes worldwide. In your research, make notes of important information for your specific tribe or culture and use these to think of unique features for your project: location, food and drink, weapons, enemies, ceremonies and more.

Seasonal Plains Indian Village

From November to March, the Plains Indians set up winter camp in protected areas with plenty of water, timber, lots of food sources and grass for their horses. In spring and summer, the Plains Indians gathered for religious ceremonies and tribal meetings. In the fall, the men gathered together for a bison hunt which gave them food and hides for the coming winter. Make a diorama showing one or all of these seasons using the Project Base & Backdrop as a display.

Suggested Materials:
- Project Base & Backdrop
- Basic Diorama Kit
- Winter Effects
- Building & Structure Kit
- Horizon & Detail Kit

Sculpt Artifacts

Pottery was used to gather water, store grains and to preserve seeds. Early pots were only functional. Later Indian pots were beautifully sculpted and decorated, as well as functional. Make your own Indian artifacts with the Sculpting Clay, Sculpting Tool, Project Paints and other materials in the Sculpting Kit.

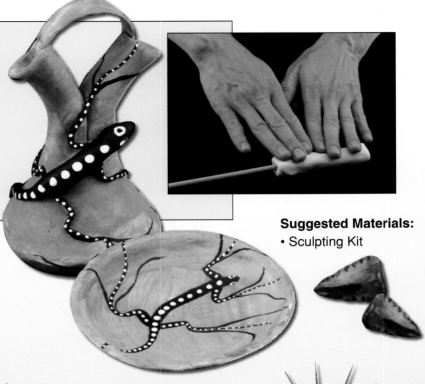

Suggested Materials:
• Sculpting Kit

Frosty Tree Tip

Take a small branch, brush on Sticky Bond and sprinkle with Snow Flakes (included in Winter Effects).

Winter Technique

Use Snow Flakes and Snow Base, included in Winter Effects, to make snowdrifts or a light dusting on your diorama.

Build a Tepee (Tipi)

Tepees were the homes of many Plains Indians and were considered a sacred place to them. Build a tepee with the Project Cloth and Project Sticks, included in the Building & Structure Kit. Show the different parts of the tepee and explain the process of building it. Or, build a diorama using the Basic Diorama Kit as the base, showing an Indian village, with lots of tepees.

Suggested Materials:
• Building & Structure Kit

Did You Know?

Basket Makers were members of an early Native North American culture in the Southwest. They covered baskets with clay and baked them hard to create waterproof containers. To recreate this technique, take a small basket and cover it with the clay from the Sculpting Kit. Let it dry and paint it with an Indian design.

Missions

There are Missions spread all over the world. In America, California Missions seem to be the most popular, though there were hundreds set up across America in the early 1800s. Most of these missions still stand as churches, and others have been made into parks. You can make replicas of missions using a Diorama Kit, Accents and Accessories.

Mission Diorama

You can build a beach or desert mission with the Desert Oasis Diorama Kit. Make copies of photos to cut out and place on your diorama. The Desert Sand ReadyGrass Sheet, included in the kit, makes a great sandy base for a beach or desert setting. Add foliage, flowers, trees and water to finish your diorama.

SAN ANTONIO DE PADUA

Suggested Materials:
• Project Base & Backdrop
• Desert Oasis Diorama Kit
• Ripplin' Water Kit
• Palm Trees

Stained Glass

Use paints and markers to color Clear Plastic (included in the Building & Structure Kit), to make stained glass.

Water Fountain

Mold Water Effects, included in the Ripplin' Water Kit, to form moving water in a fountain.

Did You Know?

The word "Alamo" comes from the Spanish word álamo, meaning cottonwood trees.

Stucco Texture

Apply Plaster Cloth and paint it for a stucco effect on your buildings.

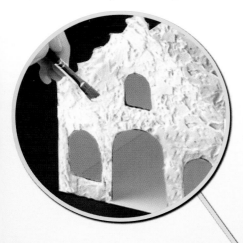

Flowering Details

Make a pot and fill it with Foliage Fiber and Red and Yellow Flowers, included in the Foliage & Grasses accent kit.

Building Details

You can make a tiled roof or floor using texture techniques and the Project Board, included in the Building & Structure Kit.

💡 **Mission San Diego de Alcalá**

MISSION SAN DIEGO DE ALCALÁ
NAME: Amy   SUBJECT: Social Studies   TOPIC: California History

Suggested Materials:
- Project Base & Backdrop
- Building & Structure Kit
- Palm Trees
- Foliage & Grasses

Though America is a baby country, compared to countries like England and Russia, a lot of history has happened! There have been wars, the advent of the railroad, great structures erected and technological advances which have built the nation. You can make dioramas, displays and other projects depicting the progress of America. There are great scenes from wagon trains moving west, Indian civilizations, military scenes, missions and much more. You'll have fun making them and learning all about history at the same time!

Santa Fe Trail Diorama

The Santa Fe Trail was a large transportation route across southwestern North America, connecting Missouri with Santa Fe, New Mexico. It was established in 1821 by William Becknell and was used as an important highway for the military and goods. Build a diorama depicting the trail and travelers in their covered wagons.

Suggested Materials:
- Project Base & Backdrop
- Desert Sand ReadyGrass Sheet
- Building & Structure Kit
- Desert Plants
- Horizon & Detail Kit

SANTA FE TRAIL PIONEERS
This scene depicts travelers in the 1820s, along the Santa Fe Trail crossing the desert in their covered wagon.

Santa Maria Ship Model

The Santa Maria was the largest ship on the Christopher Columbus voyage across the Atlantic Ocean in 1492. This model of the Santa Maria was built using the Building & Structure Kit. The sails were made from the Project Cloth, the mast from Project Sticks and the hull from Project Board, all included in the Building & Structure Kit.

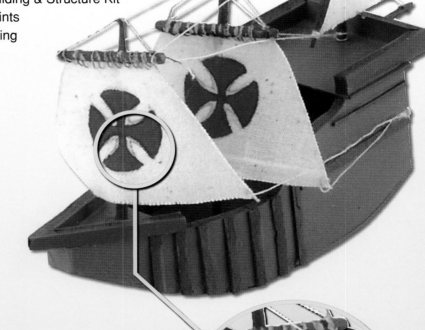

Covered Wagons

There were several types of covered wagons used by settlers. To make a specific type use Project Board, Project Cloth and Project Sticks, included in the Building & Structure Kit.

Suggested Materials:
• Building & Structure Kit
• Paints
• String

Flowering Cacti

Glue Red and Yellow Flowers, included in Desert Plants, to the tips of cacti to create flowering cactus.

Constructing Sails

Project Cloth is great for making the sails on a ship. Paint your sails to replicate a specific ship.

Did You Know?

Our second and third presidents, John Adams and Thomas Jefferson, died on the very same day (July 4, 1826), which was the 50th anniversary of the signing of the Declaration of Independence.

Historic Battle Scenes

Military scenes are easy to make and include lots of detail. You could model a historic battle scene, harsh fighting climates, or you could even show how some troops were horribly outnumbered in a battle. Don't forget details like the type of weapons they used, if animals were used in the battles or if other unique conditions existed. Remember, wars have been fought since the beginning of time: the Romans used chariots; the Civil War was fought completely with ground troops and horses; and the World Wars brought aircraft carriers and submarines.

American Revolution Diorama

Yorktown, Virginia was one of the most important landmarks of the American Revolution. Recreate the battle scene and display it on a Base. Use the Backdrop to display even more information.

AMERICAN REVOLUTION
The Battle of Yorktown (1781)

Suggested Materials:
• Project Base & Backdrop
• Green Grass ReadyGrass Sheet

Figure Tip

Sculpt your military figures with Sculpting Clay and then paint them. You can also paint figures that you already have to fit a specific scene.

Hills & Bunkers

Wad newspapers and stack them to form a hill or bunker. Cover with Plaster Cloth, paint and add foliage.

Did You Know?

In 1859, on San Juan Island, a farmer shot a pig rooting in his garden. The pig's owner wanted to arrest the farmer, and a disagreement began. Since the farmer's land was between borders of American and British-owned land, the American and British militaries were called in. The "Pig War" ended peaceably with only one casualty: the pig.

More Figure Tips

Photocopy, color and cut out figures for your diorama. Glue them to flat pieces of Sculpting Clay to add dimension.

ReadyGrass

Sticky Bond is great for attaching a ReadyGrass Sheet to the Project Base.

Timeline Idea

You can use the Backdrop as a timeline for your diorama, displaying important dates or chronological events.

By February 23, UN and American force Kuwait from Saudi Arabia. Saddam set hi oil wells on fire, which slowed down allie and he also spilled millions of gallons of oil Persian Gulf. Because of intense precision bo and highly trained allied soldiers, the Iraqi were easily overrun, the outcome was a con and swift victory, which resulted in and hundr thousands of Iraqi soldiers to surrender. It f mere 4 days for Coalition troops to liberate City and liberate the country.

Operation Desert Storm

The Coalition

The United States rallied many United Nations countries to the rescue of Kuwait. These countries included many Arab nations which breaks the tradition of pro-Arab countries allying a time of war, especially against Israel who also joined the coalition. Many unlikely countries were working together. Switzerland, who is infamous for their repetitive neutrality in WWII & II, gave financial support to the cause. The Arab country of Saudi Arabia had US troops on their same soil as that of the Muslim holy cities of Mecca and Medina.

"Achieving our goals will require sacrifice and time, but we will prevail. Make no mistake about that."
George Bush
February 1, 1991

On August 2, 1990, Saddam Hussein's army invaded the small oil filled country of Kuwait. It is a swift victory, and Iraq annexed Kuwait on the 8th of August. President Bush and the United Nations call on Saddam to immediately remove his forces. The UN passes resolution 678, calling for Saddam to withdraw by Jan. 15, 1991. He did not, and the next day American aircraft commenced bombing missions against Iraqi forces in Kuwait and also in Baghdad.

By February 23, UN and American forces move into Kuwait from Saudi Arabia. Saddam set hundreds of oil wells on fire, which slowed down allied troops, and he also spilled millions of gallons of oil into the Persian Gulf. Because of intense precision bombing and highly trained allied soldiers, the Iraqi forces were easily overrun, the outcome was a complete and swift victory, which resulted in and hundreds of thousands of Iraqi soldiers to surrender. It took a mere 4 days for Coalition troops to liberate City and liberate the country.

OPERATION DESERT STORM

Suggested Materials:
• Project Base & Backdrop
• Desert Sand ReadyGrass Sheet

Log Cabins & Medieval Castles

The Building & Structure Kit is great for making log cabins, castles, shacks, catapults, trebuchets, fences, bridges and much more. The Project Board can be manipulated to create a variety of building textures for walls and roofs. The Project Sticks can be used for trim, or for building just about any structure you can think of.

Make a Log Cabin

Add an authentic-looking log cabin to your diorama with materials and techniques included in the Building & Structure Kit. Give your log cabin texture by scoring the Project Board with a hobby knife. Paint or use a marker on the cabin and use a blackwash technique over it. The color will appear darker in the scored lines, making the cabin look weathered and aged.

Suggested Materials:
- Building & Structure Kit
- Hobby knife or scissors
- Paints or markers

Brick Texture

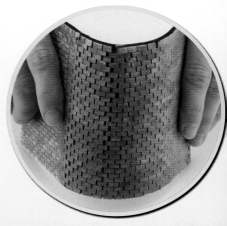

Project Board becomes flexible after it is scored and makes a great rounded tower for a castle.

ReadyGrass Road Technique

Draw the road on your ReadyGrass Sheet. Wet the turf you want to remove and scrape it away. Paint the road and add details like gravel and weeds.

Did You Know?

The highest, strongest and most secure place in a castle is called the "keep." This is where the defenders of the castle could go to watch enemies approaching the castle.

Make a Model of a Trebuchet

Trebuchets were used to hurl objects (usually rocks) great distances at approaching enemies. Build a model of a trebuchet using the materials from the Building & Structure Kit.

Suggested Materials:
• Building & Structure Kit
• Small rocks

Thatched Roof

Lay Wild Grass, included in the Basic Diorama Kit, in rows across your roof to make a thatched roof. Wild Grass is also great for bogs, haystacks and grassy meadows!

Medieval Castle

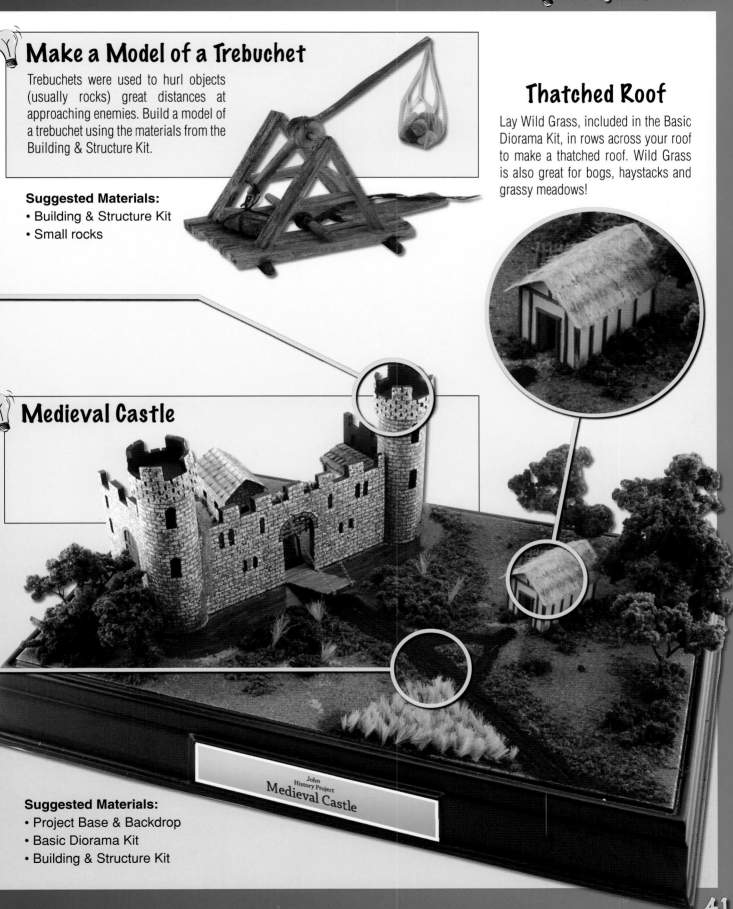

John
History Project
Medieval Castle

Suggested Materials:
• Project Base & Backdrop
• Basic Diorama Kit
• Building & Structure Kit

Ancient Pyramids

Ancient Egyptians built pyramids to bury the bodies of their dead pharaohs and queens. Pyramids are fun and easy to build, and they make great school projects. You can use the Desert Oasis Diorama Kit on a Project Base & Backdrop to build a cool diorama, then add animals like camels and sheep. You can add a river nearby with the Ripplin' Water Kit.

Inside The Great Pyramid

You can make a "cut away" pyramid to show what the inside of the Great Pyramid looks like. Use Construction Board, included in the Building & Structure Kit, to make the pyramid, showing the secret chambers, a sarcophagus, the canopic jars or a mummy inside.

Plaster Cloth Tip

Cover your pyramid with wet Plaster Cloth to give it a hard shell exterior. This will also give it some texture. Paint the Plaster Cloth after it dries.

Suggested Materials:
• Building & Structure Kit
• Plaster Cloth
• Paints

Pyramidion Tip

The cap on any pyramid is called a "pyramidion." This pyramid was painted red and topped with a golden pyramidion.

Did You Know?

Not all pyramids were built in Egypt. In terms of volume, the largest pyramid in the world is in Mexico.

The Mummy

Make a mummy using Sculpting Clay and Plaster Cloth strips. Dip the strips in water and start "wrapping" your mummy.

Egyptian Canoe

Make a canoe using Sculpting Clay from the Sculpting Kit. Paint authentic details on the side.

The Great Pyramid

Suggested Materials:
- Project Base & Backdrop
- Desert Oasis Diorama Kit
- Building & Structure Kit

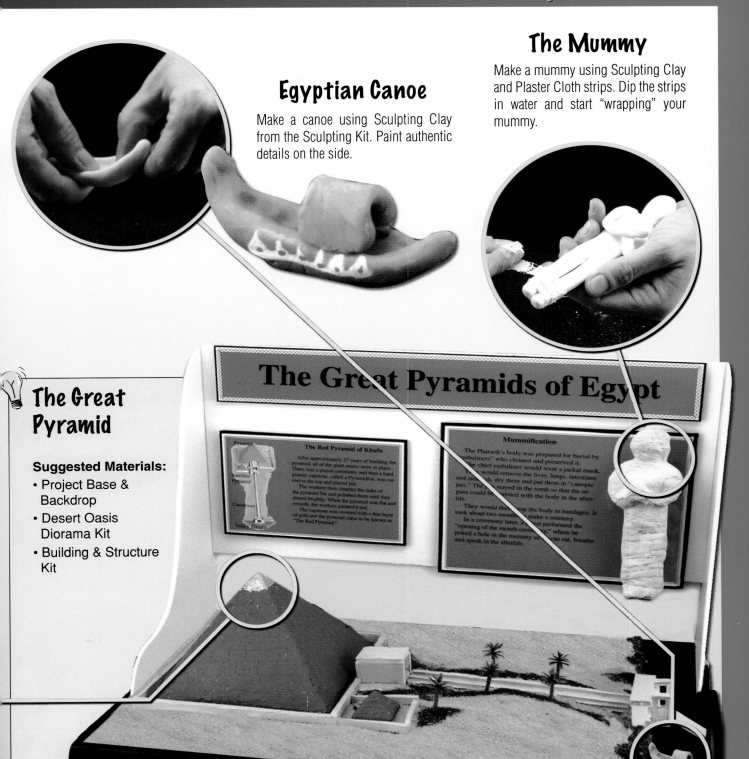

The Great Pyramids of Egypt

The Red Pyramid of Khufu

After approximately 27 years of building the pyramid, all of the giant stones were in place. There was a prayer ceremony, and then a hard, granite capstone, called a Pyramidion, was carried to the top and placed last.

The workers then chiseled the sides of the pyramid flat and polished them until they shined brightly. When the pyramid was flat and smooth, the workers painted it red.

The capstone was covered with a thin layer of gold and the pyramid came to be known as "The Red Pyramid."

Mummification

The Pharaoh's body was prepared for burial by "embalmers" who cleaned and preserved it. The chief embalmer would wear a jackal mask. They would remove the liver, lungs, intestines and stomach, dry them and put them in "canopic jars." The heart stayed in the tomb so that the organs could be reunited with the body in the afterlife.

They would then wrap the body in bandages. It took about two months to make a mummy.

In a ceremony later, a priest performed the "opening of the mouth ceremony," where he poked a hole in the mummy so it can eat, breathe and speak in the afterlife.

Great Pyramid of Khufu, 2473 B.C.
Brook Larson
5th grade Social Studies
Mrs. Rosenbach • Oak Ridge Elementary

Ancient Architecture

Many great buildings have been constructed since man came to the Earth. The Parthenon of Greece (approximately 438 B.C.), the Pantheon at Rome (approximately 27 B.C.), the Great Wall of China (approximately 228 B.C.), the Leaning Tower of Pisa and other great structures still stand as testament to the excellent, intelligent engineers and builders throughout time.

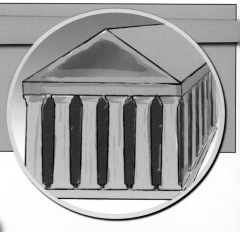

Ancient Architecture

Build realistic Greek and Roman Columns, arches, sculptures and other design elements using the Sculpting Clay from the Sculpting Kit. Add details with the Sculpting Tool and Project Paints.

Suggested Materials:
• Sculpting Kit

Backdrop Tip

Use the Backdrop to display more information. Show what Stonehenge looks like today!

ReadyGrass Tip

Glue a ReadyGrass Sheet to the base using Sticky Bond.

Did You Know?

The Circus Maximus, created by rule of Augustus in the 6th Century (B.C.), was located in Rome, and once supplied stadium seating for a quarter of a million people! It had stone bleachers, starting gates and markers around the track that counted the laps of the chariot races.

44

How Did They Do That?

Start by flattening the clay from the Sculpting Kit with a rolling pin.

Let the clay harden. This will make it easy to cut out the shapes of the stones.

Sand the pieces and paint them before adding them to your diorama.

Stonehenge

Create a small scale replica of a famous landmark and display it on the Project Base & Backdrop.

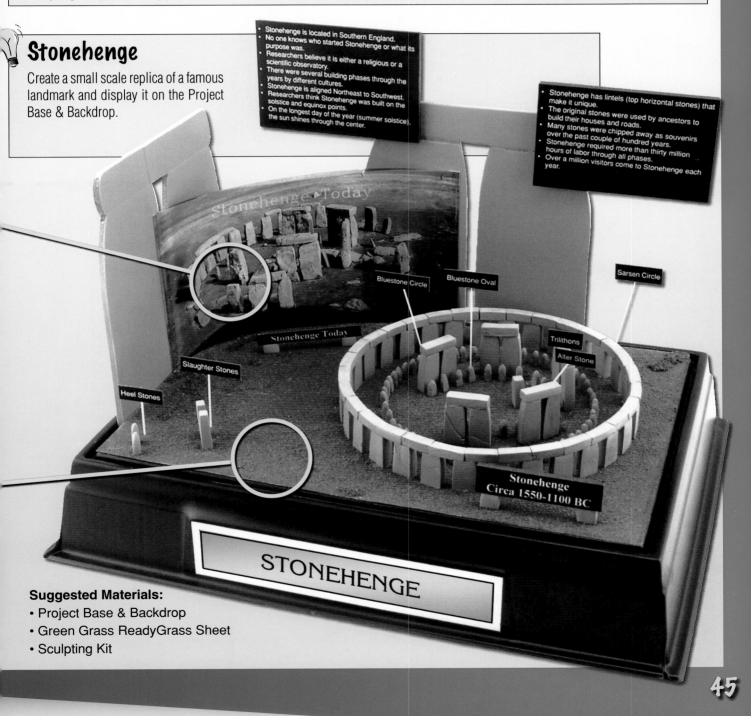

- Stonehenge is located in Southern England.
- No one knows who started Stonehenge or what its purpose was.
- Researchers believe it is either a religious or a scientific observatory.
- There were several building phases through the years by different cultures.
- Stonehenge is aligned Northeast to Southwest.
- Researchers think Stonehenge was built on the solstice and equinox points.
- On the longest day of the year (summer solstice), the sun shines through the center.

- Stonehenge has lintels (top horizontal stones) that make it unique.
- The original stones were used by ancestors to build their houses and roads.
- Many stones were chipped away as souvenirs over the past couple of hundred years.
- Stonehenge required more than thirty million hours of labor through all phases.
- Over a million visitors come to Stonehenge each year.

Stonehenge Today

Bluestone Circle

Bluestone Oval

Sarsen Circle

Trilithons

Alter Stone

Slaughter Stones

Heel Stones

Stonehenge
Circa 1550-1100 BC

STONEHENGE

Suggested Materials:
- Project Base & Backdrop
- Green Grass ReadyGrass Sheet
- Sculpting Kit

Architecture

Architecture is described as the art and science of building structure and design. There are many considerations when it comes to doing an architecture project. You could do your project on the design or the function (how the space will be used). There are many design "periods" in architecture's history, and many people design their homes and buildings on current trends. Some examples of architecture "periods" are Baroque, Neoclassical, Art Deco and Googie!

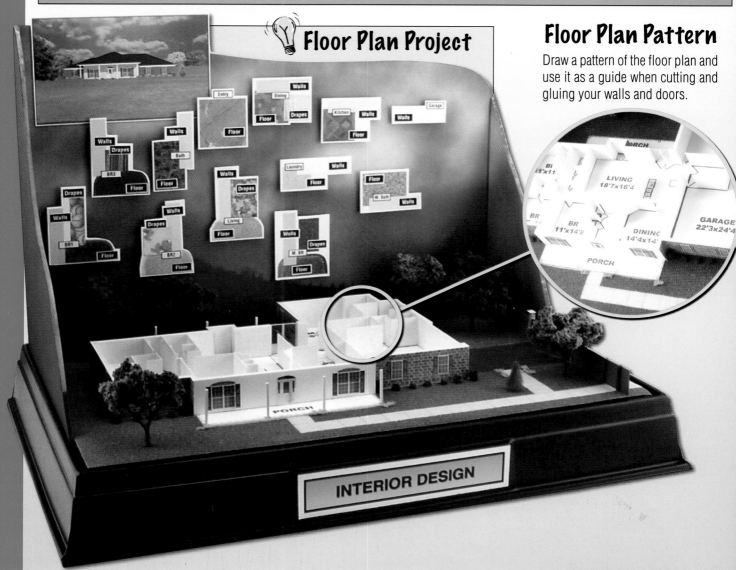

Floor Plan Project

Floor Plan Pattern

Draw a pattern of the floor plan and use it as a guide when cutting and gluing your walls and doors.

INTERIOR DESIGN

Did You Know?

The Space Needle in Seattle, Washington is an architectural marvel. According to the Space Needle Corporation, the Space Needle sways approximately 1 inch for every 10 miles per hour of wind and is approximately 1,320 Milky Way® candy bars (605 feet) tall!

Suggested Materials:
- Project Base & Backdrop
- Building & Structure Kit
- Basic Diorama Kit

Landscaping

The Water Diorama Kit includes a variety of landscaping products that are easy and fun to use, including Foliage Fiber, Green Grass, Shrubs and Evergreen and Forest Green Accents.

Architecture

Pick a famous architect and build a model of his or her structure using the Water Diorama Kit as a base.

Frank Lloyd Wright's "Fallingwater"

Frank Lloyd Wright's dream was to design homes that put the occupants close to their natural surroundings.

MODEL OF FRANK LLOYD WRIGHT'S "FALLINGWATER"

Suggested Materials:
• Project Base & Backdrop
• Building & Structure Kit
• Water Diorama Kit
• Deciduous Trees

Maps & Landscaping Projects

Topography is a geographical term which refers to the physical characteristics of the land, like mountains, hills or valleys: it is how land lays on the earth's surface. The term "relief" means to project or stand out from the surface. Relief maps of the United States show the heights and depths of the earth's surface. The Rocky Mountains are easily recognized on these maps. You can create a relief map using poster board and Plaster Cloth.

Map of the U.S.

Create a map of the United States or any country, using the Project Base & Backdrop for your display. Be sure to add a "legend" with guides for elevations, temperatures, populations and other important considerations.

Suggested Materials:
- Project Base & Backdrop
- Plaster Cloth
- Paints
- Map (optional)

Map Tip

You can resize a map on a copier or a computer and display it on the Project Base & Backdrop. Build hills and mountains with Plaster Cloth and paint it when you're finished.

Water Technique

To give your lakes, ponds, rivers and streams a realistic look, add Realistic Water over the Water Undercoat. Both are included in the Ripplin' Water Kit.

Did You Know?

Mt. McKinley in Alaska is the highest elevation in the U.S. at 20,320 feet. Death Valley in California is the lowest elevation in the U.S. at 282 feet below sea level. That is 274 feet lower than the city of New Orleans, which is eight feet below sea level!

Suggested Materials:
- Foam board
- Green Grass ReadyGrass
- Ripplin' Water Kit
- Foliage & Grasses

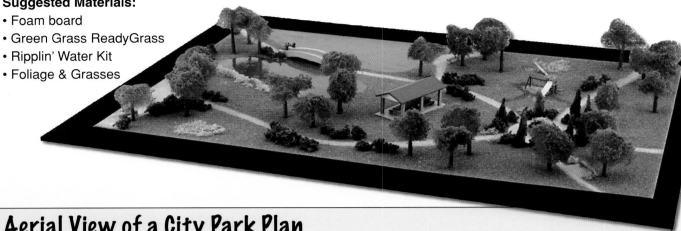

Aerial View of a City Park Plan

Mount a ReadyGrass Sheet on a piece of foam board or other sturdy backing and design your park on a flat surface. Add Realistic Water from the Ripplin' Water Kit and bushes, flowers and trees from the Foliage & Grasses accents kit. Make sure you glue everything tightly and hang it on the wall for a cool aerial view!

MEMORIAL PARK

Annie Landscape Design

49

Load-Bearing Structures

Load-bearing structures can be bridges, walls, chairs and much more. The purpose of diagramming these structures is to show how they are built and where the load is placed on the structure. Many load-bearing structures are built with simple triangles, rectangles and arches. Use the materials from the Building & Structure Kit to model almost any load-bearing structure.

Weight Distribution of a Bridge

Truss bridges can support a large amount of weight and can also span great distances because the load is distributed among many small beams. Use Project Sticks, included in the Building & Structure Kit, to construct your bridge.

The kit also includes Project Wire, Project Glue, Project Cloth, Construction Board, White Plastic, Black Paper, Project Board, Ribbed Board and Clear Plastic to finish your bridge diorama.

Pattern Technique

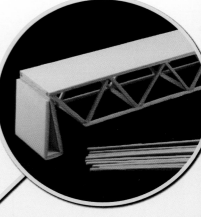

Draw a pattern of your bridge before you start to build. Lay the Project Sticks on the pattern and glue them in place to make sure all of the beams are in the right place.

HOW CONSTRUCTION AFFECTS LOAD-BEARING STRUCTURES

Girder Bridge

Girder bridges are typically built 10-200 meters across, but are harder to move to the site because of the size of the beams. In this display, because the span of the bridge is too long for the load it must bear, and there is no compression or tension support, it is sagging from the weight.

Truss Bridge

Truss bridges are made up of simple, straight beams in triangular configuration. These bridges are simple and convenient to erect, because the parts are smaller and easier to load. In this display, the bridge's triangular construction uses tension and compression to support the load, which makes it ideal for longer bridges.

400 TONS

200 TONS

SUSPENDED BRIDGE

Suggested Materials:
- Project Base & Backdrop
- Building & Structure Kit

Creative Displays

Use creative ways to display information, such as this chalkboard.

Visual Aid Tip

Start with a simple equation and use the Building & Structure Kit to create visual aids that will demonstrate the equation.

LOAD-BEARING TRIANGLES

$$h = a \sin 60° = \tfrac{1}{2}\sqrt{3}\,a$$

$$A = \tfrac{1}{2} a h = \tfrac{1}{4}\sqrt{3}\,a^2$$

$$r = \tfrac{1}{2}\, a \cot\left(\tfrac{\pi}{3}\right)$$

$$R = \tfrac{1}{2}\, a \sec\left(\tfrac{\pi}{6}\right)$$

💡 Load-Bearing Triangles

PHYSICS ASSIGNMENT
Demonstrate a Load-Bearing Structure

Suggested Materials:
• Project Base & Backdrop
• Building & Structure Kit

Book Reports

Books are great subjects for dioramas. Construct Laura Ingalls Wilder's prairie home from *Little House On The Prairie*; the Big, Bad Wolf blowing down the *Three Little Pigs* straw house; or use a ShowBox and show a scene with Alice sitting in front of the looking glass, from the book *Alice In Wonderland*. Use your imagination and do any book report you want!

Backdrop Technique

Use the Backdrop to create walls. Paint or draw lockers and bricks.

Combining Scenes

You can blend two scenes from the book together to make your diorama. Look how the soccer field and locker room scenes combine.

Book Report

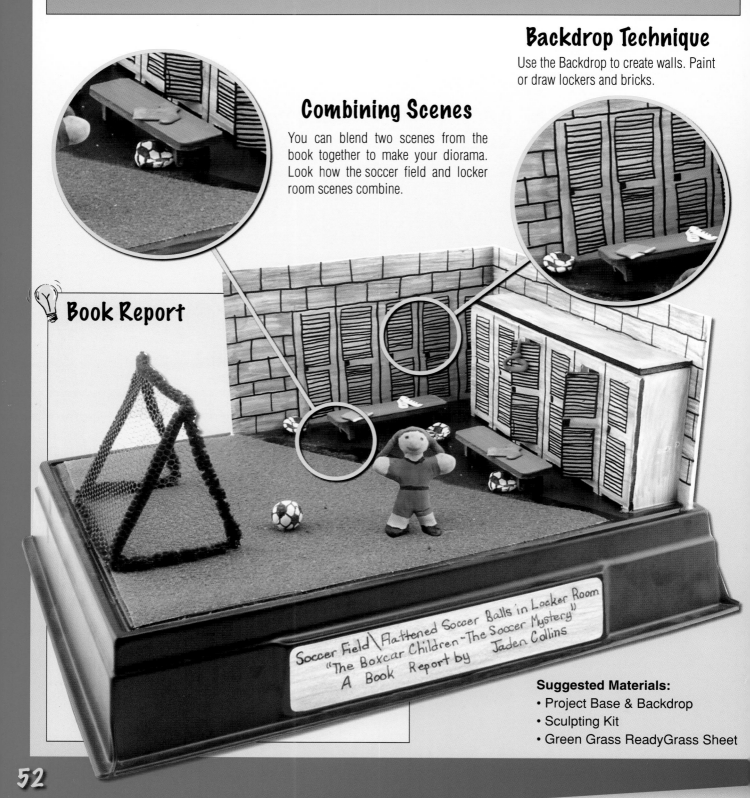

Soccer Field \ Flattened Soccer Balls in Locker Room
"The Boxcar Children - The Soccer Mystery"
A Book Report by Jaden Collins

Suggested Materials:
• Project Base & Backdrop
• Sculpting Kit
• Green Grass ReadyGrass Sheet

Board Games

Board games are easy and lots of fun to make! Use a Project Base & Backdrop, the Building & Structure Kit and Plaster Cloth to make your game in any world you wish. You could make a futuristic world game, a Science game set "in the brain" (that teaches parts of the brain), a game using your friends and their personalities, or a board game based on your favorite book or movie.

Clear Plastic Layers

Paint corn rows on Clear Plastic for a cool layered effect.

Game Construction

Use the materials in the Building & Structure Kit to make a spinner, movable pieces, buildings, bridges, tunnels and more!

💡 **Board Game**

Fairy Tale Board Game

Suggested Materials:
• Project Base & Backdrop
• Mountain Diorama Kit
• Building & Structure Kit

Storybook Shoebox Dioramas

Make a project based on a storybook. There are hundreds of books to choose from. Take your favorite scene and make a diorama using the Project Base & Backdrop or ShowBox. For instance, you could make Cinderella's carriage, with a castle painted on the Backdrop. Use the Sculpting Kit to make little mice, which are turned into coachmen. The following books would make great dioramas: *Cinderella, Rapunzel, The Three Pigs, If You Give A Mouse A Cookie, Where The Wild Things Are, Snow White, Hansel and Gretel* and *Jack and the Beanstalk*.

Storybook Shoebox Diorama

You can create storybook scenes using the ShowBox. Sculpt people, plants, houses and more with the clay from the Sculpting Kit. Use the Horizon & Detail Kit to add clouds and landscape. You can even design the outside of the box.

Suggested Materials:
• Sculpting Kit
• Horizon & Detail Kit
• ShowBox

Constructing Tip

Use the materials in the Building & Structure Kit to create floors, walls, stairs, windows and figures.

Did You Know?

In the story of Cinderella, by the Grimm Brothers, there was no fairy godmother or glass slipper. Cinderella's father was alive, and it was a little white bird, which granted Cinderella's wishes. When the prince came to find Cinderella, he brought her golden (not glass) slipper!

Important Details

Don't forget to add small, important details to your diorama to give it character. Show the grandfather clock just before the stroke of midnight and the carriage waiting in the background.

Glass Effects

You can make a glass slipper, the grandfather clock, windows and more with Clear Plastic from the Building & Structure Kit.

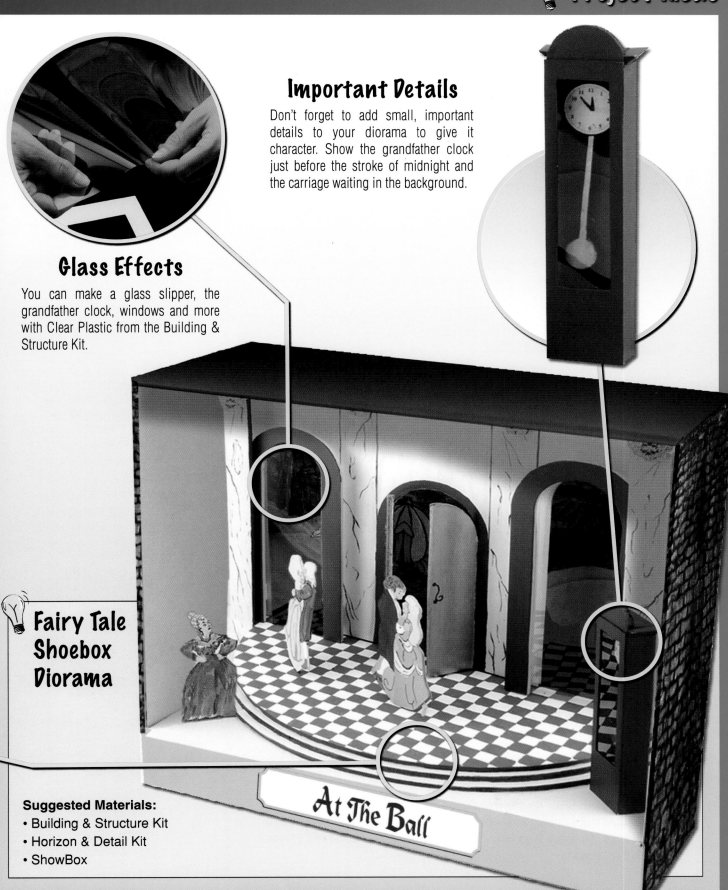

Fairy Tale Shoebox Diorama

At The Ball

Suggested Materials:
- Building & Structure Kit
- Horizon & Detail Kit
- ShowBox

Informational Displays

It only takes a little research and some imagination to make a unique display for a state project. Use the Project Base & Backdrop (or ShowBox) to begin building your display. Include things like the state flower, tree, bird, flag and motto. Don't forget to label your project!

State Project Shoebox Display

Make a display for your state using the ShowBox, the Sculpting Kit and some found objects. Roll some Sculpting Clay flat and cut out your flag. Paint it with your state colors. Sculpt your state's flower or bird. Add your state's seal and use photos of the state's tree or other state symbols to decorate your display. Include objects like the Walnut and the Dogwood branch to add to your display.

Suggested Materials:
• ShowBox
• Sculpting Kit

Preserving Leaves

Preserve leaves by breaking off a branch with leaves, then soaking the branch in a mixture of one part glycerin (available in most drug stores) and one part water. Leave the branch in the mixture for one week. Have an adult help you with this.

Display Tip

Use frames, angles and other devices to add interest to your diorama, display or project.

Did You Know?

There are more than 450 varieties of acorns. They were used as a coffee substitute during the American Civil War and now are used to fatten hogs. They are high in carbohydrates and an important source of food for wildlife.

Found Objects

When doing projects with plants or trees, gather leaves, branches, fruits and seeds from nature to add to your project.

Visual Aids Tip

Use pictures from magazines, take your own photos or draw a picture for visual aids.

💡 **Sycamore Tree**

Suggested Materials:
• Project Base & Backdrop
• Building & Structure Kit
• Paints or Markers

Sculpting, Casting & Molding

Casts can be made of anything that leaves an impression or indentation in soil, sand or other soft surfaces. Mix Casting Plaster and pour it in the impressions, then wait until it dries. Molded shapes can be made with Plaster Cloth, formed over any solid or semi-solid surface, such as a pot, balloon or other shape. Lay plastic over the shape and start adding strips of wet Plaster Cloth. Have fun smoothing the plaster with your fingers.

Be A Super Sleuth

You can cast animal, human or vehicle tracks using Casting Plaster. Go out into the woods and see what kinds of tracks you can find. Cast tire tracks just like they do on crime and mystery shows!

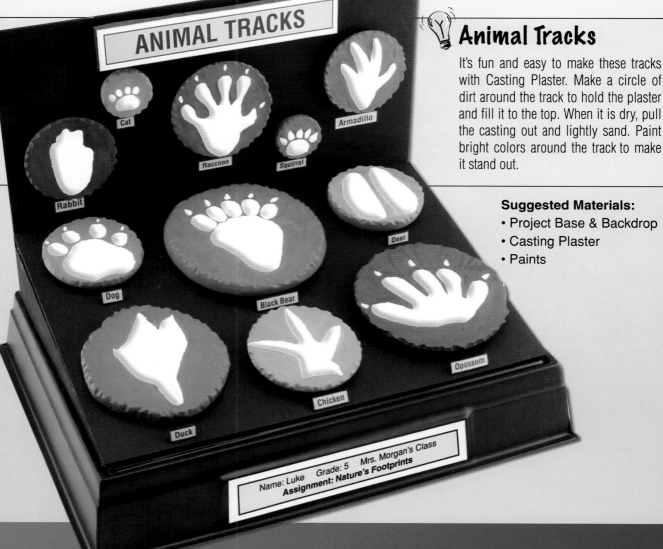

Animal Tracks

It's fun and easy to make these tracks with Casting Plaster. Make a circle of dirt around the track to hold the plaster and fill it to the top. When it is dry, pull the casting out and lightly sand. Paint bright colors around the track to make it stand out.

Suggested Materials:
- Project Base & Backdrop
- Casting Plaster
- Paints

Masks

Plaster Cloth is a versatile product that can be used to make a hard shell or a molded shape of just about anything.

💡 Special Mask Molds

You can make your own mask using your favorite Teddy Bear or doll. Cover the item with a plastic trash bag. Dip Plaster Cloth strips in water and apply over the top. Depending on the size of your project, you may need to strengthen it by applying additional Plaster Cloth. When the plaster dries, remove it and the trash bag. Trim if needed, sand the surface smooth, then paint. Add special touches from the Sculpting Kit: sculpt the bee on the end of the bear's nose, add Fun Fur and Project Paints.

Suggested Materials:
• Teddy Bear
• Medium to Large Trash Bag
• Plaster Cloth
• Sculpting Kit

Note: Never use a trash bag to cover any living thing.

Mask Mold

Be sure to cover the object with a plastic bag to keep it clean while using Plaster Cloth.

💡 Masquerade Mask

Make a masquerade mask by marking off where the mask will be and applying Plaster Cloth to that area. Trim and sand the mask before painting and decorating. Attach ribbons, a rubber band or a stick to the mask so you can wear it!

Suggested Materials:
• Mannequin or doll head
• Plastic bag
• Paints and decorations

Masks

Masks are easy and fun to make using Plaster Cloth. You can make tribal masks for school projects, fun masks for Halloween, or Mardi Gras masks to hang on your wall as a decorative interior item, or to wear to a party. Plaster Cloth dries to a hard shell surface that can be sanded, painted, cut or altered in any shape you desire. Don't forget to add decorations to make it unique.

Creative Shaped Masks

You can create your very own unique mask using Plaster Cloth and some items found around your house. For example, use a balloon, newspaper wads or a foam mannequin head as a mold. Add facial features - such as ears, a nose, a mouth or horns - using the clay from the Sculpting Kit. Apply strips of wet Plaster Cloth. Depending on the size of your project, you may need to strengthen it by applying additional Plaster Cloth. When it dries, you will have a hard shell mask to paint and decorate any way you like!

Special Touches

Add your own special touches, like yarn, sequins, feathers, beads and glitter to make your mask stand out.

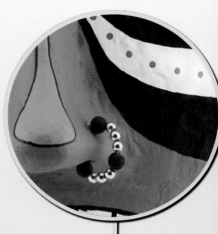

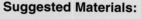

Suggested Materials:
- Newspaper
- Plaster Cloth
- Paints and decorations

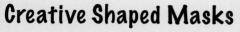

Did You Know?

Ancient masks were usually used for hunting purposes and tribal ceremonies. The earliest known mask was found in a cave in Southern France. The mask portrays a human, masked in deer skin and antlers.

💡 Easy Balloon Mask

Start with a medium-sized balloon. Sculpt features with clay from the Sculpting Kit.

Cut strips of Plaster Cloth. Dip them in water and apply over the balloon (three or more layers is recommended).

Pop the balloon. Cut, trim, sand and paint your mask.

Note: Not recommended for use directly on the face.

Suggested Materials:
- Medium-Sized Balloon
- Plaster Cloth
- Sculpting Kit (includes paints!)

💡 Display a Group of Masks

Suggested Materials:
- Project Base & Backdrop
- Plaster Cloth
- Paints and decorations

Mardi Gras

Ceremonial

Theatrical

FACE MASKS

Seasonal Projects

The changing seasons and holidays are a great time for creative displays and decor. You can make jack-o'-lanterns and masks for Halloween, snowmen and ornaments for Christmas and winter fun, plus hearts and flowers and other decorations for any time of the year. Plaster Cloth is ideal for these projects, and is so easy and fun to work with. Try it for yourself!

Easter Eggs

Creating Easter Eggs is a fun activity for the whole family that you can cherish forever! To make your eggs larger-than-life, form an oversized egg with newspaper wads and apply Plaster Cloth all around the shape. Depending on the size of your project, you may need to strengthen it by applying additional Plaster Cloth. Allow to dry, and then sand until smooth. Add

Casting Plaster over the Plaster Cloth to achieve a smoother surface. Sand, paint and decorate.

Suggested Materials:
- Plaster Cloth
- Newspaper
- Paints and decorations

Snow Flakes

Finish your snowman by covering the wet, white paint with Snow Flakes, included in Winter Effects.

Spirits Arising

Haunted House

Suggested Materials:
- Project Base & Backdrop
- Building & Structure Kit
- Summer Grass ReadyGrass
- Twigs

62

Jack-O'-Lantern

Shape newspaper wads. Use damp paper towels to make ridges. Cover with Plaster Cloth and let dry (three or more layers is recommended).

Cut the top section off with a hobby knife and pull out the newspaper wads, like pumpkin seeds and pulp.

Cut the eyes, a nose and mouth. Add Casting Plaster to fill in holes, then sand. Paint and decorate!

Plaster Cloth Snowman

Suggested Materials:
- Plaster Cloth
- Newspaper
- Paper towels
- Paints and decorations

Suggested Materials:
- Plaster Cloth
- Newspaper or balloons
- Paints and decorations

Balloon Ornaments

You can make ornaments using small balloons and Plaster Cloth. It's easy - blow up balloons, cover with Plaster Cloth (three or more layers is recommended) and allow to harden. Smooth with sandpaper and decorate!

Suggested Materials:
- Small balloon
- Plaster Cloth
- Paints and decorations

Religious Projects

The world's many different religions are full of wonderful stories which can be made into dioramas or displays. For example, there are many scenes from the *Bible* that lend themselves to making dioramas: the three crosses at Calvary, Moses parting the Red Sea, Jonah in the belly of the whale and the Nativity scene showing Jesus Christ's birth.

Nativity Scene Shoebox Diorama

Make a nativity scene for Christmas using the ShowBox, Foliage & Grasses and the Horizon & Detail Kit. Paint cut-out figures of people and animals.

Wild Grass

Use the Wild Grass, included in Foliage & Grasses, as the hay in the manger and Foliage Fiber for the roofing material.

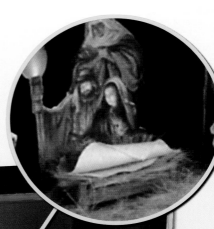

O, Holy Night

Suggested Materials:
- ShowBox
- Horizon & Detail Kit
- Foliage & Grasses

The Ark

Build the hull of Noah's Ark with the Project Board from the Building & Structure Kit.

Rainbow

Use the Project Paints, included in the Horizon & Detail Kit to paint your rainbow background and other details. Use the acronym, ROY G BIV, to put your rainbow colors in order: red, orange, yellow, green, blue, indigo and violet!

💡 Noah's Ark

Create a diorama of your favorite *Bible* story on the Project Base & Backdrop. Sculpt your own animals and figures with the Sculpting Kit.

Suggested Materials:
• Project Base & Backdrop
• Building & Structure Kit
• Sculpting Kit
• Horizon & Detail Kit

40 *Days* & 40 *Nights*

Displays, Easels & Shadowboxes

Build a display to showcase your winning derby car, model cars or airplanes with the Project Base & Backdrop. Shadowboxes are also a fun way to display things that are important to you. If you collect rocks or arrowheads, these are very easy to display.

Racer Display

Create a display for your PineCar Derby® racer using a Project Base & Backdrop and ReadyGrass Sheet. Add raceday journaling or a photo of you with your car!

Suggested Materials:
- Project Base & Backdrop
- Green Grass ReadyGrass Sheet

Make an Easel

Make an easel to prop up your shadowbox using the Project Base & Backdrop.

Saving Materials

Use the scraps from the cut Backdrop to make pedestals, frames and other decorative items for your display.

I WON THE PINECAR DERBY!
Linn Creek Derby Daredevils Challenge
February 22, 2007

1st Place Award

Jimmy and I tied three times before my Muscle Racer zoomed by Jimmy's car and I won!!!

Craftsmanship Award

Dad let me do all of the work, but he did help me a little with the band saw. It was cool! Everyone said my car looked the best ...even Jimmy!

Mark, Grade: 5   SHOW & TELL PROJECT

How Did They Do That?

 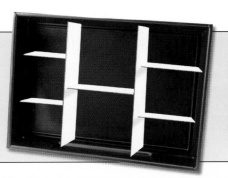 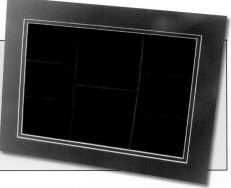

Start with the Project Base. Flip it over so the inside area is facing you.

Measure and cut pieces of the Backdrop to fit the inside base. Glue into place with Project Glue.

Paint the inside pieces to match the base and frame with matte board.

Seashell Shadowbox

Shadowboxes aren't just for collections of similar items. Make a collage of your summer vacation, including brochures, photographs, small souvenirs, sand from the beach and much more!

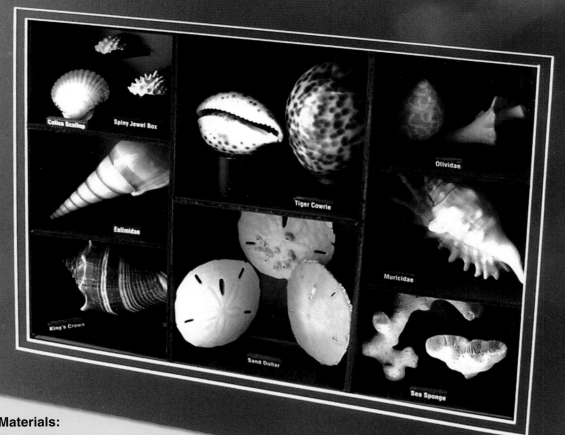

Suggested Materials:
- Project Base & Backdrop
- Matte board
- Black paint

About Building Basics

The following pages include building basics to help you build dioramas with unique detail. Specific instructions are included in each Scene-A-Rama kit.

Project Base & Backdrop Basics

Project Base & Backdrop Options

Use the Project Base & Backdrop in these configurations, or make up your own. The Backdrop can be used in various ways to suit any project, diorama, display or shadowbox.

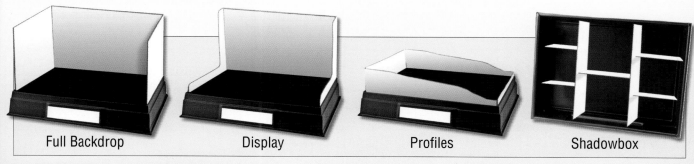

Full Backdrop   Display   Profiles   Shadowbox

Setting Up Your Base & Backdrop

The Backdrop fits in the groove of the Base and can be used to hide the unfinished edges of your project. You may want to wait until your project is finished before taping it in place.

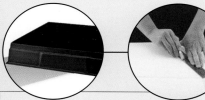   

| Plan your project and test fit the Backdrop. | If desired, cut Backdrop with a hobby knife. Add paint or labels. | When ready to attach, apply double-sided tape to the Backdrop. | Place the Backdrop in the groove. |

Basic Dioramas

Making a Display with a ReadyGrass Sheet

The Basic Diorama Kit and Desert Oasis Diorama Kit include a ReadyGrass Sheet for easy ground coverage. ReadyGrass Sheets can also be purchased individually.

| Apply Sticky Bond. | Let glue set until clear. Place on Base. | Add foliage, trees, flowers and more. | Place Backdrop in groove. |

MEADOW

Mountain Dioramas

Building With Side Panels

The Mountain Diorama Kit and Water Diorama Kit include Side Panels which allow you to build mountains, volcanoes and hills.

Cut Side Panels and tape on Base.	Use newspaper wads to build mountains.	Cover newspaper with Plaster Cloth.	Add rocks, foliage, trees and more.	Place Backdrop in groove around Side Panels.

Basic Rock Making, Installing & Coloring

Making Rocks

The Rock Making Kit and Mountain Diorama Kit include everything to make rocks, including Casting Plaster, Mixing Tray, Rock Colors and a Rock Mold.

Mix Casting Plaster.   Stir until blended.   Pour into Rock Molds.   Pop rocks out when dry.

Installing Rocks

The Rock Making Kit and Mountain Diorama Kit also include everything you need to install and color rocks (with the unique Leopard-Spotting Technique), including Project Glue, Rock Colors and Foam Brush.

Test fit rock.   Add Project Glue to back of rock.   Place rock and let dry.

Coloring Rocks with the Leopard-Spotting Technique

Dab Yellow Rock Color on rock with Foam Brush.   Rinse brush and dab Brown Rock Color on rock. Rinse brush.   Dab Black Rock Color over rock and allow to dry.   Color area around rock, add foliage, Talus and water.

Basic ReadyGrass Techniques

Make a Paved Road
Add roads to ReadyGrass Sheets. The turf can be easily removed and painted.

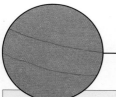

Mark the area where you want to remove the turf.	Wet the marked area.	Scrape the turf away.	Paint the road area and let dry.

Add Talus, Shrubs and rocks to the sides of the road.

Making Rocks with ReadyGrass Sheets
Create three-dimensional rocks from a flat piece of paper!

Wad newspaper into a rock shape.	Wrap ReadyGrass Sheet around wad.	Glue and hold in place with rubberband.

Basic Tree Making Techniques

Making Trees with Tree Armatures (or sticks)
The Basic Diorama Kit includes Tree Armatures and foliage for making Deciduous Trees. You can also use sticks instead of Tree Armatures.

Twist armatures.	Apply Sticky Bond.	Dip into foliage.

Place trees on diorama.

Making Trees With Foliage Fiber
Conifers are easy to make with Foliage Fiber and Evergreen Accents, included in the Mountain Diorama Kit, Water Diorama Kit and Foliage & Grasses.

Cut Foliage Fiber.	Stretch Foliage Fiber.	Spray tree with Project Glue.	Sprinkle with Evergreen Accents.

Place trees on diorama.

Basic Water Techniques

Make a Waterfall

The Ripplin' Water Kit and the Water Diorama Kit have everything you need to make waterfalls, including Water Effects and Release Paper.

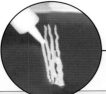  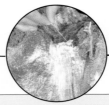 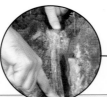

| Pour Water Effects on Release Paper. | Spread with toothpick. | Set in place. | Blend with Water Effects. |

Make a Body of Water

The Ripplin' Water Kit and the Water Diorama Kit also include Realistic Water, Foam Brush, Stir Stick and Water Undercoat for making bodies of water.

   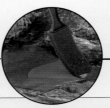

| Draw water area. | Paint Water Undercoat. | Pour Realistic Water. | Spread water evenly. | Add surrounding scenery. |

Basic Wild Grass Techniques

Planting Wild Grass

Wild Grass, included in the Desert Oasis Diorama Kit, Foliage & Grasses and Desert Plants, is great for tall grasses, thatched roofs and more.

| Trim Wild Grass. | Dip in Project Glue. | Plant on diorama. |

Add a thatched roof to your building.

Basic Winter Weather Techniques

Dusting of Snow, Snow Drifts, Icy Ponds & Icicles

Winter Effects contains everything you need to make cold-weather effects, including Snow Flakes, Snow Base, Stir Stick, Release Paper and Ice Effects.

  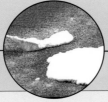 

| Sprinkle Snow Flakes for a dusting. | Mix Snow Flakes and Snow Base into paste. | Spread paste to make snowdrifts. | Spread Ice Effects to form icicles. | Add effects to houses and roads. |

Basic Plaster Cloth Techniques

Making Round Shapes

Balloons make it easy to shape round or oval shapes. Just add Plaster Cloth around it.

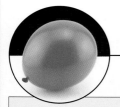   

Start with a small balloon.	Add features with Sculpting Clay.	Cover with wet Plaster Cloth*.	Allow to dry, then sand and paint.

Making Irregular Shapes

Wet Plaster Cloth can be molded over any form. When it dries, the form stays, like this scarf.

Drape Plaster Cloth over newspaper.	Allow to dry until hard.	Sand for a smooth surface.

Finish by painting and decorating.

Depending on the size of your project, you may need to strengthen it by applying additional Plaster Cloth (three or more layers is recommended).

Basic Sculpting Techniques

Sculpting Dolphins, Fish & Other Animals

The Sculpting Kit includes Sculpting Clay, a Sculpting Tool, Paints and other sculpting materials.

Roll clay into ball. Shape into dolphin body.	Pinch and pull a top fin and the tail.	Roll two small tubes, then flatten to make flippers.	Wet clay to attach. Smooth if needed.

Sculpting Structures

The Sculpting Clay hardens into a perfect surface for cutting, trimming and engraving.

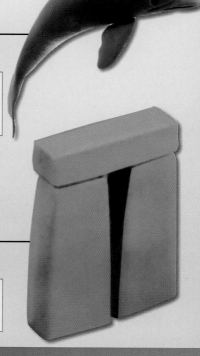

Roll Sculpting Clay flat.	Allow to dry until hardened.	Cut pieces with hobby knife.	Sand pieces with sandpaper. Paint.

Basic Painting Techniques

Use paint to create different textures and effects for your dioramas and displays. *Drybrush* for a weathered look, *sponge* for a raised surface effect, *blend* for transitions between colors surfaces and *blackwash* for an antique finish.

Drybrushing

Dab paint-filled brush on paper towel until nearly dry and brush over surface.

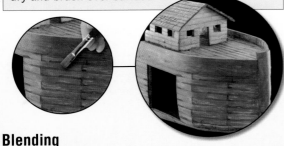

Sponging

Lightly dab sponge on surface repeatedly, making a textured pattern.

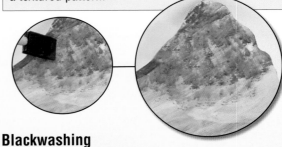

Blending

Softly blend wet paint colors together with brush.

Blackwashing

Mix black paint with water. Cover entire object with mixture. Dab with paper towel.

Basic Framing & Labeling Techniques

Make a Frame

The Building & Structure Kit contains a variety of framing and labeling materials.

Measure your photograph.	Cut Project Board to wrap around photo.	Score the corners of the frame.	Bend the frame and glue into place.

Labeling

Print or draw labels and mount them on Project Board. Use the Project Wire included in the Horizon & Detail Kit, Building & Structure Kit or Sculpting Kit to suspend your labels.

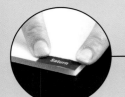

Glue to Project Board.	Cut out labels.	Paint the edges.	Mount with wire.

Basic Buildings

Make a Log Cabin

The Building & Structure Kit contains Project Board, which is great for making buildings and structures with texture and dimension.

   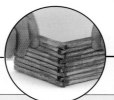 

Draw pattern on Project Board.

Cut out pattern with a hobby knife.

Texture walls and roof then paint.

Assemble pieces and glue together.

Add chimneys, windows, doors and other details.

Make a Pyramid

Use the Building & Structure Kit with other materials, like Plaster Cloth, to create cool effects.

Draw a pattern on Project Board.

Cut out the pyramid with a hobby knife.

Fold into a pyramid and glue or tape.

Cover with wet Plaster Cloth.

Let dry and paint.

Simple Structures

Make a Tepee

The Building & Structure Kit includes Project Cloth and Project Sticks that work well together.

   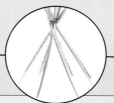 

Draw a tepee pattern on Project Cloth.

Cut out the pattern and paint the cloth.

Tie the Project Sticks on one end and fan the other end.

Wrap cloth around sticks. Glue in place.

Make a Bridge

Use Project Sticks to construct any kind of structure and hold it together with Project Glue.

    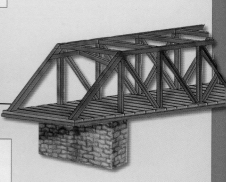

Draw your bridge pattern.

Place, measure and cut Project Sticks.

Glue the bridge together with Project Glue.

Assemble the rest of the bridge.

Basic Building Textures

You can make a wide variety of building textures with simple techniques, such as scoring, indenting and scratching the Project Board and Ribbed Board, included in the Building & Structure Kit.

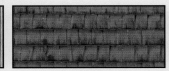
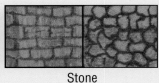

Bricks   Corrugated Metal   Shingles   Stone

Cinder Blocks   Siding   Logs   Terra-Cotta Clay

Castle Brick Wall

Make rounded castle towers with Project Board from the Building & Structure Kit.

Cut castle walls from Project Board.

Use a hobby knife to score walls in a brick pattern.

Assemble and then paint.

More Textures

Use Plaster Cloth for stucco, Wild Grass for thatched roofs and Foliage Fiber for moss roofs to create more unique building textures. These products are included in various kits.

Stucco   Thatched Roof   Moss Roof

Stucco Mission

Plaster Cloth makes a great stucco texture for the exterior of your mission.

Build a mission.

Cover with wet Plaster Cloth.

Pinch Plaster Cloth to make it bumpy.

Paint the dry Plaster Cloth.

Project Base & Backdrop

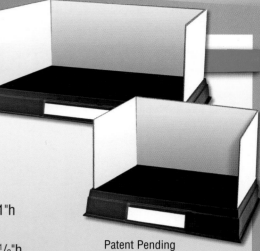

Project Bases come in two sizes: large and small. They can be modified to make shadowboxes and have a built-in placard for labeling your project. The included Backdrops are great for backgrounds, horizons or labeling project parts. Also includes labels and double-stick tape for easy assembly.

Project Base & Backdrop Large
Overall Size: 18"w x 12 $\frac{1}{2}$"d x 13 $\frac{1}{8}$"h Project Area: 16 $\frac{1}{4}$"w x 10 $\frac{3}{4}$"d x 11"h

Project Base & Backdrop Small
Overall Size: 12 $\frac{1}{2}$"w x 9 $\frac{1}{4}$"d x 9 $\frac{5}{8}$"h Project Area: 10 $\frac{3}{4}$"w x 7 $\frac{3}{8}$"d x 7 $\frac{1}{2}$"h

Patent Pending

ShowBox™

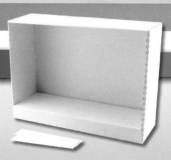

The ShowBox is great for shoebox dioramas. It is constructed of sturdy, white material. Paint, decorate, label or use the box as is. Labels included.

Overall Size: 13 $\frac{1}{2}$"w x 4 $\frac{1}{2}$"d x 10"h Inside Dimensions: 13"w x 4 $\frac{1}{2}$"d x 8 $\frac{1}{2}$"h

Trees

Add realistic, ready-to-use trees and watch your diorama or display come to life!

Deciduous Trees   **Conifer Trees**   **Palm Trees**   **Autumn Trees**

ReadyGrass® Sheets

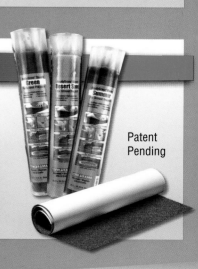

Attach to Project Base to represent grass or sand. Available in three colors (10 $\frac{3}{4}$" x 16 $\frac{1}{4}$" sheets).

Patent Pending

Summer Grass   **Green Grass**   **Desert Sand**

Building & Structure Kit

Create buildings, structures, geometric shapes and more. Kit contents:

- Project Boards
- Project Cloth
- Project Sticks
- Clear Plastic
- Construction Board
- White Plastic
- Black Paper
- Ribbed Board
- Project Wire
- Project Glue
- Easy Instructions

Sculpting Kit

Make figures, animals and shapes for your projects. Includes paints, tools, tips and techniques. Kit contents:

- Sculpting Clay
- Sculpting Tool
- Project Paints
- Paintbrush
- Fun Fur
- Project Wire
- Project Glue
- Easy Instructions

Horizon & Detail Kit

Make horizons and backgrounds. Includes cloud and mountain-making materials. Kit contents:

- Plaster Cloth
- Project Paints
- Foliage Fiber
- Green Grass
- Puffy Clouds
- Project Wire
- Paintbrush (1/2")
- Paintbrush (1/8")
- Project Glue
- Easy Instructions

Plaster Cloth & Casting Plaster

Use Plaster Cloth to make masks, hard land surfaces, ornaments and more. Forms over almost any shape!

Use Casting Plaster to cast rocks, fossils, tracks and more, just like the crime scene labs! Use with any mold or impression.

Project Glue & Sticky Bond®

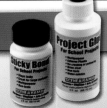

Project Glue is a multipurpose, water-soluble adhesive. Safe for kids.
Sticky Bond is great for bonding ReadyGrass Sheets to Project Bases. Stays tacky.

Diorama Kits

The four Diorama Kits include all the materials you need to make any environment for your project. They can be built on a Project Base & Backdrop or any surface. Create your choice of a basic landscape, a mountain or volcano, a water scene or a desert oasis.

Basic Diorama Kit

This kit includes a ReadyGrass Sheet for an instant, grassy flat area for buildings and habitats. Use the included bushes, grasses, flowers and your imagination to create more. Kit contents:

- Green Grass ReadyGrass
- 6-Tree Armatures
- Foliage Fiber
- Shrubs
- Wild Grass
- Yellow Flowers
- Evergreen Accent
- Forest Green Accent

- Sticky Bond
- Project Glue
- Spray Bottle
- Foam Brush
- Sifter
- Stir Stick
- Easy Instructions

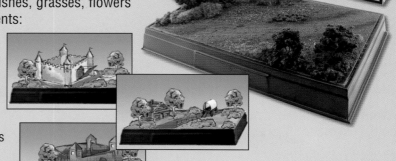

Mountain Diorama Kit

Make mountains, volcanoes, hills, caves, erosion or land contours with rock outcroppings. Create any scene with included earth-colored paint, grasses, bushes, soils, vines and rock debris. Kit contents:

- Earth Undercoat
- Rock Colors
- Volcano Tube
- Shrubs
- Foliage Fiber
- Green Grass
- Evergreen Accent
- Forest Green Accent
- Rock Mold
- Casting Plaster

- Talus
- Side Panels
- Plaster Cloth
- Project Glue
- Spray Bottle
- Mixing Tray
- Foam Brush
- Sifter
- Stir Stick
- Easy Instructions

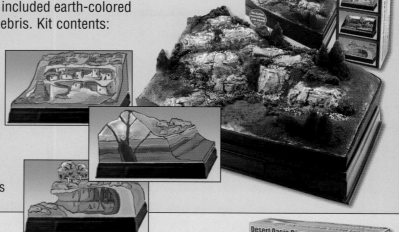

Desert Oasis Diorama Kit

Create a desert oasis scene! Use for missions, beaches and much more. Includes palm trees, desert vegetation, short and tall grasses, flowers, sand, rocks and vines. Kit contents:

- Desert Sand ReadyGrass
- 5-Palm Trees (4"- 5")
- Foliage Fiber
- Wild Grass
- Green Grass
- Yellow Flowers
- Talus
- Sticky Bond

- Project Glue
- Spray Bottle
- Foam Brush
- Sifter
- Stir Stick
- Easy Instructions

Water Diorama Kit

Make and color still or moving water scenes, such as lakes, rivers or waterfalls. Add the included landscaping: earth-colored paint, short and tall grasses, bushes and vines. Kit contents:

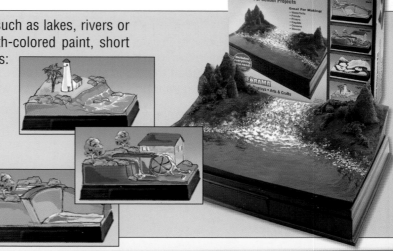

- Realistic Water
- Water Effects
- Water Undercoat
- Earth Undercoat
- Side Panels
- Plaster Cloth
- Shrubs
- Foliage Fiber
- Green Grass
- Evergreen Accent
- Forest Green Accent
- Talus
- Project Glue
- Spray Bottle
- Foam Brush
- Sifter
- Stir Stick
- Release Paper
- Easy Instructions

Accents

Use these kits to enhance your diorama or display. Add foliage and grasses, rocks, water, desert plants and winter effects. They give your project that added detail. If you imagine it...you can build it!

Dioramas shown built with additional Scene-A-Rama products.

Rock Making Kit

Learn how to use a Rock Mold to create a multitude of rock formations with Casting Plaster. Kit contents:

- Rock Mold
- Casting Plaster
- Rock Colors
- Talus
- Mixing Tray
- Foam Brush
- Stir Stick
- Project Glue
- Easy Instructions

Ripplin' Water Kit

Create lakes, rivers, waterfalls, rapids, waves and more. Kit contents:

- Realistic Water
- Water Effects
- Water Undercoat
- Foam Brush
- Stir Stick
- Release Paper
- Easy Instructions

Foliage & Grasses

Add bushes, shrubs, flowers, weeds and grasses to a diorama. Kit contents:

- Foliage Fiber
- Bushes
- Green Grass
- Forest Green Accent
- Yellow Flowers
- Project Glue
- Wild Grass
- Spray bottle
- Sifter
- Easy Instructions

Desert Plants

Includes cacti, flowers, grasses and brush. Kit contents:

- Saguaro Cacti
- Columnar Cacti
- Prickly Pear Cacti
- Barrel Cacti
- Red Flowers
- Yellow Flowers
- Wild Grass
- Foliage Fiber
- Project Glue
- Easy Instructions

Winter Effects

Create realistic heavy drifts or light dustings of snow for your diorama, display or project. Kit contents:

- Ice Effects
- Snow Flakes
- Snow Base
- Foam Brush
- Sifter
- Stir Stick
- Release Paper
- Easy Instructions

Project Packs

Build models like the professionals! Project Packs are perfect for creating school projects, building science and art fair displays, producing museum-quality dioramas or just having fun on a rainy day! With the included materials and a little creativity, you will be amazed at the ease of designing and building your project and the fun you will have in the process.

- School Projects
- Science & Art Fair Displays
- Museum Quality Dioramas
- Rainy-Day Fun

Erupting Volcano

Creative Mask & More

Native American Village

Cell Structure

Classroom Packs

For today's teacher! Scene-A-Rama™ Classroom Packs contain everything you need to build projects that will engage students in the lesson, reinforce what they've learned and create an educational environment that's fun! These projects are designed to aid students in meeting national education standards.

- Each pack contains enough material for 12 projects, including teacher and student guides
- Each project has been classroom-tested to ensure success
- How-to videos and fun photos that correspond with each project are available at www.scenearama.com

Tepee Village

Erupting Volcano

Creative Mask

Cell Structure

Scene-A-Rama™ is a division of:
Woodland Scenics® – The World Leader in Model Scenery

Woodland Scenics created the Scene-A-Rama product line especially for students!

We've made it fun and easy for kids who are creating school projects. Each Scene-A-Rama product is easy to use and ASTM certified*. But please don't stop with only the kits and accents offered in the Scene-A-Rama product line. These are only the beginning of realism, beauty and versatility you can achieve!

Woodland Scenics offers more than 1,000 individual scenery products!

With our comprehensive scenery and accessories, you can build larger dioramas with a wide variety of colors and textures, awesome figures, vehicles and buildings.

You don't have to be an artist to achieve beautiful dioramas!

Take it from Woodland Scenics (the experts in model scenery) and the satisfied customers over the years: you can make a diorama as simple or as elaborate as you wish.

This is an actual model using Woodland Scenics products.

With Woodland Scenics it will always come out beautifully!

We specialize in products for model railroading, architectural model building, wargaming, collectible house displays and other hobbies. Fine art museums, major motion picture and network studios (and top production studios) all around the world use our products! Look for quality Woodland Scenics products in your local hobby shop or visit our fun Web sites at **www.woodlandscenics.com** and **www.scenearama.com.**

WOODLAND SCENICS®

*All Scene-A-Rama products conform to ASTM D4236 Health Requirements.

81

Scene-A-Rama/Woodland Scenics Product Conversion Chart

Many Scene-A-Rama components can be purchased from Woodland Scenics. Woodland Scenics has a wide variety of textures, colors and landscaping items for scenery. Use the chart below to correspond the Scene-A-Rama product with the comparable Woodland Scenics product. Go to the Web site **www.woodlandscenics.com** to look at all you can do with Woodland Scenics!

Scene-A-Rama Product	Product Included in These Kits	Woodland Scenics Product	Product Number
Realistic Water	Water Diorama Kit, Ripplin' Water Kit	Realistic Water	C1211
Water Effects	Water Diorama Kit, Ripplin' Water Kit	Water Effects	C1212
Rock Colors	Mountain Diorama Kit, Rock Making Kit	Earth Colors (Yellow Ocher, Burnt Umber & Black)	C1223, C1222, C1220
Rock Molds	Mountain Diorama Kit, Rock Making Kit	Rock Molds	C1230-C1244
Tree Armatures	Basic Diorama Kit	Tree Armatures	TR1120-1125
Foliage Fiber	Foliage & Grasses, Desert Plants, Basic Diorama Kit, Mountain Diorama Kit, Water Diorama Kit, Desert Oasis Diorama Kit, Horizon & Detail Kit	Poly Fiber	FP178
Talus	Mountain Diorama Kit, Water Diorama Kit	Talus (Brown or Natural)	C1274, C1283
Wild Grass	Foliage & Grasses, Desert Plants, Basic Diorama Kit, Desert Oasis Diorama Kit	Field Grass (Gold or Green)	FG172, FG174
Shrubs	Basic Diorama Kit, Mountain Diorama Kit, Water Diorama Kit	Clump-Foliage (Medium Green)	FC683, FC183
Bushes	Foliage & Grasses	Bushes (Dark Green)	FC147, FC1647
Evergreen Accents	Basic Diorama Kit, Mountain Diorama Kit	Weeds Fine Turf	T46
Green Grass	Mountain Diorama Kit, Water Diorama Kit, Desert Oasis Diorama Kit, Horizon & Detail Kit	Green Grass Fine Turf	T45
Yellow Flowers	Foliage & Grasses, Desert Plants, Basic Diorama Kit, Desert Oasis Diorama Kit	Fall Yellow Coarse Turf	T1353
Red Flowers	Desert Plants	Fall Red Coarse Turf	T1355
Earth Undercoat	Mountain Diorama Kit	Earth Undercoat	C1229
Snow Flakes	Winter Effects	Soft Flake Snow	SN140
Ice Effects	Winter Effects	Realistic Water	C1211

Scene-A-Rama Product	Product Included in These Kits	Scene-A-Rama Product	Product Number
Project Glue	Foliage & Grasses, Rock Making Kit, Desert Plants, Basic Diorama Kit, Mountain Diorama Kit, Water Diorama Kit, Desert Oasis Diorama Kit, Building & Structure Kit, Sculpting Kit, Horizon & Detail Kit	Project Glue	SP4142
Sticky Bond	Basic Diorama Kit, Desert Oasis Diorama Kit	Sticky Bond	SP4143
Plaster Cloth	Mountain Diorama Kit, Water Diorama Kit, Horizon & Detail Kit	Plaster Cloth	SP4140
Casting Plaster	Mountain Diorama Kit, Rock Making Kit	Casting Plaster	SP4141
Summer Grass ReadyGrass	N/A	Summer Grass ReadyGrass	SP4160
Green Grass ReadyGrass	Basic Diorama Kit	Green Grass ReadyGrass	SP4161
Desert Sand ReadyGrass	Desert Oasis Diorama Kit	Desert Sand ReadyGrass	SP4162
Deciduous Trees	N/A	Deciduous Trees	SP4150
Conifer Trees	N/A	Conifer Trees	SP4151
Palm Trees	Desert Oasis Diorama Kit	Palm Trees	SP4152
Autumn Trees	N/A	Autumn Trees	SP4153
Snow Base	Winter Effects		
Puffy Clouds	Horizon & Detail Kit		
Volcano Tube	Mountain Diorama Kit		
Water Undercoat	Water Diorama Kit, Ripplin' Water Kit		
Forest Green Accents	Foliage & Grasses, Basic Diorama Kit, Mountain Diorama Kit		
Sculpting Clay	Sculpting Kit		
Fun Fur	Sculpting Kit	Check back for product availability.	
Release Paper	Water Diorama Kit, Ripplin' Water Kit		
Project Board	Building & Structure Kit		
Clear Plastic, Construction Board, Project Cloth, Project Sticks, Black Paper, Ribbed Board	Building & Structure Kit		
Side Panels	Mountain Diorama Kit, Water Diorama Kit		
Project Wire	Building & Structure Kit, Sculpting Kit, Horizon & Detail Kit		
Project Paints	Sculpting Kit, Horizon & Detail Kit		

Consider these additional Woodland Scenics products for your project: Premium Trees™ (preassembled, distinctive trees); **Ready Made Realistic Trees** (economical); **Dead Fall** (dead timber); **Flowering Foliage** (for flowering vines and trees); **Fruit** (for fruit trees); **Scenic Accents®** (figures, animals, accessories); **Built-&-Ready® Structures** (preassembled buildings); **AutoScenes®** (vehicle and accessories that tell a story); and **Decals** (signs, letters, numbers and more).